DESIGN
FOR HOW PEOPLE
LEARN

JULIE DIRKSEN

New Riders

VOICES THAT MATTER™

DESIGN FOR HOW PEOPLE LEARN, SECOND EDITION

Julie Dirksen

New Riders

Find us on the Web at www.newriders.com
New Riders is an imprint of Peachpit, a division of Pearson Education.
To report errors, please send a note to errata@peachpit.com

Copyright © 2016 by Julie Dirksen

Acquisitions Editor: Nikki Echler McDonald
Production Editor: Maureen Forys, Happenstance Type-O-Rama
Development Editor: Margaret S. Anderson, Stellarvisions
Copy Editor: Scout Festa
Proofer: Steffi Drewes
Compositor: WolfsonDesign
Indexer: FireCrystal Communications
Cover Design: Mimi Heft
Interior Design: Danielle Foster

ISBN 13: 978-0-134-21128-2
ISBN 10: 0-134-21128-6

9 8 7 6 5 4 3 2 1

Printed and bound in the United States of America

ACKNOWLEDGMENTS

There are many, many people I'm grateful to, including:

The really smart people who, through reviews, help, feedback, and contributions, made this book much better than it would otherwise have been: Brian Dusablon, Chris Atherton, Connie Malamed, Dave Ferguson, David Kelly, Debbie Gjerde, Jane Bozarth, Janet Laane Effron, Jason Willensky, Jeremy Beckman, Jessica Snively, Judy Katz, Mark Britz, Sarah Gilbert, Simon Bostock, Steve Howard, Tracy Hamilton Parish, Trina Rimmer, and Trish Uhl. Thank you so much.

All the marvelous Peachpit/New Riders folks. Until I started on this project, I had no idea how many talented and skilled professionals are involved in creating a book like this. Thank you all for your hard work. Thanks in particular to Margaret Anderson, Nikki McDonald, Scout Festa, and Steffi Drewes (2nd edition) as well as to Wendy Sharp, Susan Rimerman, Becky Winter, and Wendy Katz (1st edition).

All of my colleagues who have provided lots of advice, ideas, and interesting conversations, including Aaron Silvers, Allison Rossett, Andy Petroski, Cammy Bean, Carla Torgerson, Cathy Moore, Chad Udell, Charles Palmer, Clark Quinn, Craig Wiggins, Dan Thatcher, David Bael, Edmond Manning, Ellen Wagner, Ethan Edwards, Francis Wade, Justin Brusino, Karl Fast, Karl Kapp, Kevin Thorn, Koreen Pagano, Laura Nedved, Lester Shen, Lyle Turner, Maria Haverhals Andersen, Matt Taylor, Megan Bowe, Nadine Pauw, Reuben Tozman, Rick Raymer, Steve Flowers, Stevie Rocco, Tom Kuhlmann, Wendy Wickham, Will Thalheimer, and Zen Faulkes. Also to some of the smart people whose work has so informed my own understanding: Amy Jo Kim, Dan Lockton, Dustin DiTommaso, Sebastian Deterding, and Stephen Anderson, along with everyone on the inspiration bookshelf. Also Marty Siegel and the IST program at Indiana University.

My beautiful friends and family who have listened and supported: Margaret Hanley, Lori Baker, Lisa Boyd, Samantha Bailey, Kathleen Sullivan, Tesia Kosmalski, Michele McKenzie, Rebecca Davis, Angela Eaton, and Ann Woods. Also my honorary "aunts" Sandra Schurr and Lenore Dupuis.

And my family (Eric, Tessie, and Jonathan) and my parents, who were very supportive (and a little concerned) when I said, "I think I'm going to quit my job and freelance so I can work on a book." It seems to be working out so far.

Finally, thanks to the mentors who have so informed my own thinking and practice: Michael Allen and Kathy Sierra. This book couldn't exist without your examples, ideas, and inspiration.

CONTENTS

INTRODUCTION

Think about the best learning experience you've ever had. What was it like?

Got one? I've asked this question dozens of times and gotten a variety of answers. Sometimes the answer is that someone was really passionate about what they were learning, but the most frequent answer is:

Nobody ever says, "I had the most amazing textbook" or "There was this *really great* PowerPoint deck!"

That suggests that a lot of what makes for a great learning experience is not about the content but about the way the content is taught. In fact, a class can cover the same material but be very different, depending on how the material is taught:

Tedious textbook + excellent teacher = Amazing!

Tedious textbook + OK teacher = Meh.

So what's the special sauce? How are the two experiences different? When it's two different teachers, some of the differences are due to personality or charisma, but those aren't usually the only differences. And when it's an elearning course, there's no teacher at all. How is a really good elearning course different from just reading a textbook online?

Even more important, what's the difference between a learning experience that's effective and one that gets forgotten as soon as the learner is done? Even "amazing" classes are useless if the learner doesn't do something different afterward. While some learning experiences are "learning for the sake of learning," I won't really address those in this book. (Disclaimer: I work with adult learners, usually in a professional setting, so while the book will address examples from multiple contexts, the majority will relate to adult workplace learning experiences.)

For me, the goal of good learning design is for learners to emerge from the learning experience with new or improved capabilities that they can take back to the real world and that help them do the things they need or want to do. If your learners are on a journey from novice to expert, how can you help them along that path?

This book looks at some of the things involved in designing great learning experiences:

Chapter 1: Where Do We Start?
If learning is a journey, what's the gap between where they are and where they need to be? Sometimes that gap is knowledge, but just as often the gap can be skills, motivation, habit, or environment.

Chapter 2: Who Are Your Learners?
Your learners see the world differently than you do, and to design effective learning experiences you need to understand their view of the world.

Chapter 3: What's the Goal?
The best learning experiences are designed with a clear destination in mind. Learn how to determine your destination with accuracy.

Chapter 4: How Do We Remember?
Learn about how the brain works to focus on and retain information.

Chapter 5: How Do You Get Their Attention?
Learn strategies for getting past the distractions and helping your learners focus their attention.

Chapter 6: Design for Knowledge
The most common type of learning experience focuses on teaching knowledge. Learn strategies to make this as effective as possible.

Chapter 7: Design for Skills
Skills require practice. Learn strategies for helping your learners get the practice they need to develop those skills.

Chapter 8: Design for Motivation
If you've ever heard a learner say the words "I know, but..." then you are probably dealing not with a knowledge gap but with a motivation gap. Learn strategies for getting your learners to not only learn more but also do more.

Chapter 9: Design for Habits
Sometimes the gap isn't knowledge or skill or even motivation, but is rather a question of habits.

Chapter 10: Social and Informal Learning
When is formal learning *not* the answer? Learn about social and informal learning options.

Chapter 11: Design for Environment
Sometimes it's better to fix the environment rather than the learner.

Chapter 12: Designing Evaluation
After you build a learning experience, how do you know whether it works? Learn ways to evaluate and assess learning.

WHERE DO WE START?

(IN WHICH WE LEARN THAT IT'S NOT ALWAYS ABOUT WHAT PEOPLE KNOW, AND THAT YOU SHOULDN'T USE A SUSPENSION BRIDGE TO FIX A POTHOLE)

THE LEARNER'S JOURNEY

Are the following statements true or false?

- If you teach people about how smoking is bad for them, they'll stop smoking.
- If someone reads a management book, that person will be a good manager.
- If someone takes a really good web design class, that person will be a good web designer.
- If you teach people the right way to do something, they won't do it the wrong way.

Did you think any of those statements were completely true?

No, of course you didn't, because there are a lot of complicating factors that influence whether a person succeeds or not.

Learning experiences are like journeys. The journey starts where the learner is now, and ends when the learner is successful (however that is defined). The end of the journey isn't just knowing more, it's *doing* more.

So if the journey isn't just about knowing more, then what else is involved? What else needs to be different in order for someone to succeed?

WHERE'S THE GAP?

There's a gap between a learner's current situation and where they need to be in order to be successful. Part of that is probably a gap in knowledge, but as we began to discuss above, there are other types of gaps as well.

If you can identify those gaps, you can design better learning experiences.

For example, consider the following situations. What could be the gaps for each of these scenarios?

- **Alison** is a project manager for a web design company, and she's just agreed to teach an undergraduate project-management class at a design school. Her students will mostly be students in the second year of the creative design program. Most of the students are 18 or 19 years old and are taking the class because it's a requirement for their degree.
- **Marcus** is teaching a two-day workshop on database design for a new database technology. This is the second time he's taught the workshop, and he's revising it because it was too basic the first time around.
- **Kim** is designing a series of elearning courses for a large global company that recently merged with a smaller company. The two companies are buying a new purchasing system to replace the older systems. The employees of the smaller company will also need to learn the procedures from the larger company.

For each of these, think about how the learner should be different—what could and should they do differently—before and after the learning experience?

In the case of Alison's class, it could be that the gap is just a matter of knowledge: A student comes in not knowing anything about project management, and comes out knowing a lot more about project management.

But is a lot of project management knowledge all that's needed to make somebody a capable project manager? There's more to good project management than just knowing information. And of course that will hold true for much more than Alison's class. Let's take a closer look at knowledge, or information, gaps, and then talk about what other types of gaps can exist for learners.

KNOWLEDGE GAPS

Information is the equipment your learners need to have in order to perform. Having information doesn't accomplish anything by itself. Something is accomplished when the learner *uses* that information to do things.

Basically, you want your learners to have the right supplies for their journey:

You also want your learners to know what to *do* with that information. Having the information without knowing how and when to use it is like having a really great tent that you don't know how to put up or spending a lot of money on a really terrific camera but still taking cruddy pictures because you don't have the abilities needed to use it.

If the *only* thing your learner is missing is the information, then your job is actually pretty easy, especially living in this information age. There are lots of easy, cheap ways to convey information.

Another benefit of the information age is that you don't necessarily need your learners to carry all the information the whole way on their journey. If they can pick up less critical information as they go along, you can focus initially on the more critical knowledge that they really need to have with them the whole way.

As for all the rest of that information, think about how you can cache it for your learners so that they can easily pick it up when they need it. If they get the information when they really need it, they'll also appreciate it more.

We'll take a closer look at different ways to supply information to your learners in later chapters.

IS IT REALLY A KNOWLEDGE GAP?

There's a common tendency to assume that the gap is information—*if the learner just had the information, then they could perform.*

I recently worked with a client on a project to teach salespeople how to create a product proposal for potential clients. The salespeople need to be able to:

- Choose which product best meets a client's needs
- Select a series of options so that the product is optimally customized for that client

We were working on revising an old course in which there were four slides that simply listed each of the product features.

And that was it. Hmm.

If you were learning this, do you think this equation adds up?

No, of course not—even if the learners memorized the exact information on each of those slides, that wouldn't mean they would be able to use it well. But certainly it is always critical to start by providing the right information to the learner.

Right info   Practice   Skills   Attitude   Competent Salesperson

SKILL GAPS

Let's say I've figured out the starting point and ending point of my journey, I've got it all mapped out, and I have all the gear I need: Am I now ready to hit the 2000-mile Appalachian Trail?

Probably not.

Anything more ambitious than a gentle afternoon hike is probably beyond me at the moment. So what would I need to be ready to tackle the Appalachian Trail? Would more gear help? More route planning?

Not really. The only thing that is going to get me ready for a major, multi-day hike is a lot of hiking, and even a less ambitious goal would require practice and conditioning.

Time spent on practice devices like elliptical machines or stairclimbers would probably help toward the goal of a major hike; tackling an expert-level hike would require a lot of practice on less challenging hikes. Even if I sat down and memorized an Appalachian Trail guidebook, it still wouldn't be a good idea to try it without the necessary conditioning and skills.

Learners in all disciplines are frequently in this situation. They get handed the knowledge in a book or a class but don't get the opportunity to practice and develop skills.

Skill vs. Knowledge

Having a skill is different from having knowledge. To determine if something is a skill gap rather than a knowledge gap, you need to ask just one question:

Is it reasonable to think that someone can be proficient without practice?

If the answer is no, then you know you are dealing with a skill, and your learners will need practice to develop proficiency.

Here's a little game you can play to help you in your planning: Let's play Skill/Not a Skill:

Action	Skill?	
Saving a file in MS Word	Yes	No
Playing volleyball	Yes	No
Giving performance reviews	Yes	No
Filling out a timesheet	Yes	No
Calming an irate customer	Yes	No
Building a database	Yes	No
Designing a brochure	Yes	No
Making mac & cheese from the box	Yes	No
Problem-solving a missing supply order	Yes	No
Programming the shopping cart widget for a website	Yes	No

I don't really think that saving a Microsoft Word file, filling out a timesheet, or making macaroni and cheese would be considered skills (although you might be able to convince me on the last one), but I believe everything else on the list would require practice to do well. Some of these skills are more complex than others, requiring judgment and the ability to adapt to circumstances.

Just as you would never expect someone to tackle the Appalachian Trail on their first hiking trip, you can't expect learners to pick up new skills without practice. To teach skills, that practice must be part of the learning journey you design.

MOTIVATION GAPS

If somebody knows what to do but chooses not to do it, that's a motivation gap.

There are a number of reasons for motivation gaps:

Sometimes the person doesn't really buy into the outcome or destination.

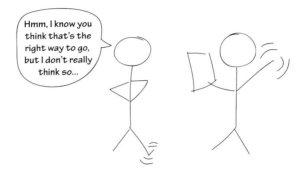

Sometimes the destination really doesn't make sense.

Sometimes it is due to anxiety, or concern about change.

Sometimes people get distracted or unfocused.

Sometimes people just aren't interested in making the effort.

Sometimes people fail because they lack enough of the big picture to guide their own success.

I was recently talking with a colleague about learner motivation, and she argued that it wasn't the learning designer's problem. She felt that people brought their own motivation to the table and that it really wasn't in the designer's control. My colleague is correct that you can't force a learner to be motivated, but as designers there are ways we can help support motivation in a learning experience. Design decisions influence people's behavior.

For example, in a recent study (Song 2009), people were given lists of tasks. The only difference between the two lists was the font used, one of which was easier to read. Participants were asked to rate how easy or difficult they thought the task would be to perform.

Tasks presented in the easier-to-read font were rated by the participants as being easier to perform. The group given the same list in a hard-to-read font rated those tasks as being harder to perform.

Lie on your back with knees bent and feet resting on a flat surface.	*Lie on your back with knees bent and feet resting on a flat surface.*
Cross arms over your chest or clasp them behind your head.	*Cross arms over your chest or clasp them behind your head.*
Tuck your chin against your chest.	*Tuck your chin against your chest.*
Tighten your abdominal muscles and curl up.	*Tighten your abdominal muscles and curl up.*

This is just one example of a fairly subtle way of influencing a learner's motivation, and paradoxically, some research suggests that things read in a harder-to-read font may be easier to remember.

There are countless decisions you might make while designing a learning experience that will influence your learner's motivation. For example, in your content, do you dwell on all the things that can go wrong? That might be a good way to prepare the learner for troubleshooting, but might also convince them that it's not worth the effort in the first place.

UNLEARNING: THE SPECIAL MOTIVATION GAP

One of the things you may need to consider in your learner's journey is whether the new learning is going to require doing something familiar in a new manner. If people are required to change the way they do things, then they are going to stumble over old habits. If they automatically do certain things, they are going to have to make a conscious effort to *not* do those things—a process called *unlearning*. This is more difficult than just making a conscious effort to do something new, and, not unimportantly, it can make people grumpy.

When Tiger Woods changed his golf swing, his game would take a hit for a while until it (usually) improved again. This is a fairly difficult process for an athlete, because it not only involves adding the new technique but also requires unlearning the old technique.

As we gain proficiency in something, the memories around that proficiency become streamlined in our brains. We get progressively more efficient in how we access and use the information and perform the procedures around that task. This is an important part of learning—if it didn't happen, then riding a bike for the thousandth time would be just as difficult and exhausting as riding a bike for the first time.

This streamlining process is a natural blessing for learning, but it poses a difficulty for *re-learning*. When learners must change or replace an existing practice, you have to deal with the fact that your learners already have *momentum*. They are already going in a particular direction, at a pretty good clip. And they have many parts of the process automated.

AUTOMATIC PROCESSES: When you automate something, you relegate control of that task to a part of the brain that doesn't require much conscious attention.

When a task is new it requires a lot of brain resources. When you are first learning to ride a bike, for example, you need to put a good amount of your conscious attention on the task of staying upright.

When you become proficient, you don't have to consciously think things like "I'm tipping! Omigosh, whaddoIdo? WhaddoIdo?" Instead, your body just adjusts left or right without your having to think about it, and you can concentrate on other important thoughts like "Oh #$%ˆ@! That log wasn't there the last time I came down this route!"

This has significant implications for learning.

Let's go back to our example with Kim from the beginning of the chapter.

SCENARIO: LEARNING NEW PROCEDURES

Kim is designing a series of elearning courses for a large global company that recently merged with a smaller company. The two companies are buying a new purchasing system to replace the older systems. The employees of the smaller company will also need to learn the procedures from the larger company.

Who do you think is going to have a bigger challenge learning the new system—the group accustomed to the existing procedures or the group learning the new procedures?

—TAKE A MOMENT TO CONSIDER HOW YOU WOULD ANSWER BEFORE MOVING ON—

Although both groups are probably going to struggle with the new computer system, employees from the smaller company will also have the extra challenge of learning a procedure that replaces the one they are used to. ▪

Old information and procedures *get in the way* of new information and procedures. Have you ever noticed that when someone is not a native speaker of your language, the word order in their sentences can be a little weird? This is called L1 interference: Your knowledge of your first language interferes with your ability to speak a second language.

If you are asking your learners to change an existing practice, you are probably going to have some motivation issues to contend with. In those instances, there are a couple of things to be aware of.

First, change is a *process*, not an event. You absolutely cannot expect someone to change based on a single explanation of the new practice. They need time and repetition to ease back on the old habit and start cultivating the new one.

Second, backsliding and grumpiness are part of that process—they don't mean that the change has failed (although that can happen too), but they are frequently an unavoidable part of even successful changes.

HABIT GAPS

Sometimes, people have the knowledge, skills, and motivation and there *still* may be a gap. For example, a new manager can have seen the importance of giving good feedback, have learned a method for giving feedback, and truly believe that it's an important thing to do, and—even after all that—still struggle to give feedback when needed. Because it's not a habit.

For most of us, a large percentage of our day is habit-driven. When I get up in the morning, probably the first half hour of my day is on auto-pilot (let the dog out, make coffee, brush teeth, etc.).

The difficulty with habits as a gap is that most of the traditional learning solutions have only mixed results at best. Have you ever said any of these?

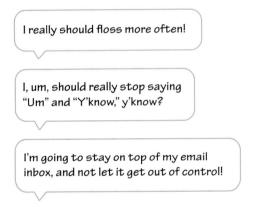

If you ever have, you know that they fall firmly into the "easier said than done" category—as do most habits, whether they're new habits to be learned or old habits to be unlearned. As a result, habits need a different learning approach, which we will discuss in a later chapter.

ENVIRONMENT GAPS

Let's say your learner has good directions, is fully prepared, is in good shape, and is raring to go. Nothing should stop them now, right?

Sometimes the path itself isn't set up to let people succeed:

Environment gaps, or challenges, can take different forms in an organization. For example, if you want somebody to change a behavior, does the process support it?

Are there materials, references, and job aids to support the learner when they get back to their work environment?

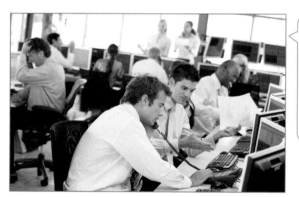

Do they have everything they need in terms of materials, resources, and technology?

Are people being incentivized and rewarded for making the change?

Is the change being reinforced over time?

COMMUNICATION GAPS

Sometimes a failure to perform is due not to a lack of knowledge but to bad directions or instructions.

This isn't really a learning issue—this is a case of miscommunication. It can happen for all sorts of reasons. Sometimes, the person communicating the direction doesn't really know where they want people to go; they don't know the goal.

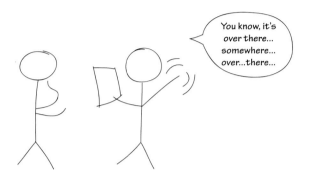

Or sometimes, the person communicating knows where they want people to go but can't adequately communicate that knowledge.

Occasionally, the person giving the directions says one thing, but either doesn't support it or really intends something else.

For example, let's say that one of Alison's students is using all his shiny new project-management abilities on building a website for his uncle, but a few weeks into the project, it's not going very well.

The website is behind schedule, the person doing the graphics can't finish them, and the design for the whole gallery section is a mess.

Does that mean that Alison's student didn't really learn everything he needed to know about project management? Maybe he's making rookie mistakes, despite everything he learned in class?

Or could it be that the uncle is the client from hell who didn't say that he was leaving the country for a month, changes his mind frequently, and forgot to mention that he wanted a gallery section on the website in any of the initial meetings? That might be why.

So how much of this is a learning issue? None of it, really, but communication issues can sometimes masquerade as learning issues.

We need training to improve the level of customer service.

We're getting killed on the customer satisfaction surveys.

But the surveys say that what they are really unhappy about is that they spend 10 minutes on hold, and wind up in loops in the automated phone system.

Um, customer service training won't actually fix any of that...

Frequently, the best you can do in those situations is document the issue, handle the politics, and do no harm to the learners, if possible.

IDENTIFYING AND BRIDGING GAPS

So when you are mapping out the route, you need to ask yourself what the journey looks like.

Knowledge

- What information does the learner need to be successful?
- When along the route will they need it?
- What formats would best support that?

Skills

- What will the learners need to practice to develop the needed proficiencies?
- Where are their opportunities to practice?

Motivation

- What is the learner's attitude toward the change?
- Are they going to be resistant to changing course?

Habits

- Are any of the required behaviors habits?
- Are there existing habits that will need to be unlearned?

Environment

- What in the environment is preventing the learner from being successful?
- What is needed to support them in being successful?

Communication

- Are the goals being clearly communicated?

Questions to Ask

There are a variety of strategies to help identify the gaps. Here are a few for starters:

- Ask "What do they actually need to *do* with this?" (If you get the answer "They just need to be aware of it," then ask "Yeah, but what do they actually need to *do* with this?" *again.*)
- Follow a novice around and watch what they do; then follow an expert around and ask "What are they doing differently?"
- Ask yourself if the person *would be able to* do something if they wanted to badly enough. If the answer is yes, it's not a knowledge or skills gap.
- Ask the question "Is there anything—anything at all—that we could do, besides training, that would make it more likely that people would do the right thing?"
- Ask "Is this going to involve changing the way they do things now?"
- Ask "What is the consequence if somebody does it wrong?"
- Ask "If someone is getting this exactly right, what would that look like?"
- Ask "Is it reasonable to assume that someone will get this right the first time out, or will they need to practice to get proficient?"

EXAMPLES

Let's identify the gaps in a few scenarios.

SCENARIO 1: MARIANNA

Marianna is a newly minted supervisor for her company's IT support department. She was a great IT support person and now she's been promoted, supervising five other IT support workers.

Her HR department sends her to a new-manager training class, where she learns all about the paperwork necessary for managing hourly workers, and about a coaching model for providing good and timely feedback to her direct reports.

Marianna's first few weeks are a bit rocky. She is swamped by the paperwork demands, and has to work really hard to keep up. Other supervisors seem to stay on top of their paperwork, so Marianna isn't really sure what she's doing wrong. A couple of her employees are starting to come in late, and she's reluctant to confront them directly about it, because she doesn't want it to seem like she got all bossy just because she was promoted. She tries to use the coaching method she was taught, but although it works a little with one of the problem employees, it doesn't work at all with the other. As Marianna gets busy, she doesn't really finish all the steps to the coaching process. She's not that convinced it was helpful anyway.

Marianna's manager is aware that she's struggling somewhat, and is thinking of arranging more managerial training for her.

Which of the following gaps are relevant for Marianna?

- Knowledge
- Skills
- Motivation and attitude
- Habit
- Environment
- Communication

—TAKE A MOMENT TO CONSIDER HOW YOU WOULD ANSWER BEFORE MOVING ON—

This is almost certainly not a knowledge problem. Marianna appears to know *what* to do, but she needs a lot more guided practice to develop the skills that will help her perform the task efficiently and well. She has some attitude (self-confidence) and motivation gaps that make her reluctant to use what she knows. Specific coaching from her manager will probably be more helpful than additional classes, and it's possible that there are elements in her environment that could be changed to help her keep up with the paperwork.   ■

SCENARIO 2: MARCUS

Let's revisit Marcus, from the beginning of the chapter, and take a closer look at his situation.

Marcus is teaching a two-day workshop on database design for a new database technology. This is the second time he's taught the workshop, and he's revising it because it was too basic the first time around. It was kind of a rough first teaching experience for Marcus.

Originally, he spent a lot of time on the principles of database design and got out his old textbooks to cover basic design principles such as how to normalize a database.

When he taught the class, though, it turned out that most people in the class were actually experienced database designers who were there specifically to learn the new technology. Some of the students complained about the functionality of the technology, and Marcus felt unprepared when students wanted him to explain *why* things had to be done a particular way.

Which gaps does Marcus need to think about for his audience?

- Knowledge
- Skills
- Motivation and attitude
- Habit
- Environment
- Communication

—TAKE A MOMENT TO CONSIDER HOW YOU WOULD ANSWER BEFORE MOVING ON—

His first time around, Marcus focused more on database design skills, which his audience didn't really need. His audience does have a knowledge gap around the functionality of the new system, and there are some attitude/motivation gaps that are likely the product of his learners being forced to do things differently than they are accustomed to. If Marcus can focus on getting his audience comfortable with the specific software functionality and how it can be useful for them, his second class will probably go better. ▪

SCENARIO 3: ALISON

Let's also revisit Alison from the beginning of the chapter.

Alison, a project manager for a web design company, has just agreed to teach an undergraduate project-management class at a design school. Her students will mostly be students in the second year of the creative design program. Most of the students are 18 or 19 years old and are taking the class because it's a requirement for their degree.

Which gaps does Alison need to think about for her audience?

- Knowledge
- Skills
- Motivation and attitude
- Habit
- Environment
- Communication

—TAKE A MOMENT TO CONSIDER HOW YOU WOULD ANSWER BEFORE MOVING ON—

There's no indication of a communication issue, but Alison will need to accommodate pretty much all of the other types of gaps. Her students don't have a lot of work experience to draw on, and probably don't have much or any project-management knowledge. They will need to develop skills to be able to apply what she teaches, and will need to have elements in their environment to support what they learn. Given that it's a required course, and that her students are primarily art and design students, she needs to think about how to encourage their attitude and motivation.

WHY THIS IS IMPORTANT

Several years ago, I was working on a proposal for a prospective client. The client had come to the company I worked for and said, "We have a problem with a high employee turnover rate. We want a training course on the history of the company to reduce that rate."

We gently suggested that if they had a high turnover rate, it was probably not primarily due to employee ignorance of company history, and would they like us to look into other possible causes?

Yeah, we didn't get that contract. Oh darn.

In Chapter 3, we'll take a look at how to set good goals for learning, but before you get to goals, it's really important to define the gap you are trying to fill or the problem you are trying to solve.

If you don't start with the gaps, you can't know that your solution will bridge them. You can build a suspension bridge to cross a crack in the road, or try to use a 20-foot rope bridge to span the Grand Canyon.

One of my all-time favorite clients was a group that did drug and alcohol prevention curriculums for middle-school kids. When they were initially explaining the curriculum to me, they talked about how a lot of earlier drug-prevention curriculums focused on information ("THIS is a crack pipe. Crack is BAD.").

Now does anyone think the main reason kids get involved with drugs is a lack of knowledge about drug paraphernalia, or because no one had ever bothered to mention that drugs are a bad idea?

Instead, this group focused on practicing the heck out of handling awkward social situations involving drugs and alcohol. Kids did role-plays and skits, and brainstormed what to say in difficult situations. By ensuring that the curriculum addressed the real gaps (e.g., skills in handling challenging social situations), they were able to be much more effective.

If you have a really clear sense of where the gaps are, what they are like, and how big they are, you will design much better learning solutions.

SUMMARY

- A successful learning experience doesn't just involve a learner knowing more—it's about them being able to *do* more with that knowledge.
- Sometimes a learner's main gap is knowledge, but more frequently knowledge and information are just the supplies the learner needs to develop skills.
- Use the question "Is it reasonable to think that someone can be proficient without practice?" to identify skills gaps. If the answer is no, ensure that learners have opportunities to practice and develop those skills.
- You need to consider the motivations and attitudes of your learners. If they know how to do something, are there other reasons why they aren't succeeding?
- Change can be hard because learners may have deeply ingrained patterns or habits they have to unlearn, and you need to expect that as part of the change process.
- The environment needs to support the learner. People are much less likely to be successful if they encounter roadblocks when they try to apply what they've learned.
- Sometimes it's not a learning problem, but rather a problem of communication, direction, or leadership. Recognizing those instances can save a lot of effort in wrong directions.
- If you have a well-defined problem, you can design much better learning solutions. It's always worth clearly defining the problem before trying to define the solution.

REFERENCES

Ellickson, Phyllis, Daniel McCaffrey, Bonnie Ghosh-Dastidar, and Doug Longshore. 2003. "New Inroads in Preventing Adolescent Drug Use: Results from a Large-Scale Trial of Project ALERT in Middle Schools." *American Journal of Public Health*. 93(11): 1830–6.

Song, Hyunjin and Norbert Schwarz. 2009. "If It's Difficult to Pronounce, It Must Be Risky." *Psychological Science* 20 (2): DOI: 10.1111/j.1467-9280.2009.02267.

WHO ARE YOUR LEARNERS?

(IN WHICH WE LEARN THAT OUR LEARNERS ARE NOT NECESSARILY LIKE US, AND ALSO THE IMPORTANCE OF TIDY CLOSETS)

Understanding your learners is part of designing good learning experiences. If you don't understand your learners, unfortunate things can happen.

So what do you want to know about your users? First of all, you might want some basic demographic information (such as age, gender, job, or role). You can usually get that information via a survey, or sometimes organizations already have that kind of data on file.

You may also want to know things like their reading level or how they use technology, if those things are relevant to the subject you are working on. You can also use surveys to find those things out, or you can talk to some representative learners (which is always a good idea).

In addition to those types of audience demographics, you also want to get the answers to a few key questions:

- What do your learners *want*?
- What is their current skill level?
- How are your learners different from you?

We'll look at these questions in this chapter. Additionally, we'll take a look at learning styles, and also what methods you should use to gather the information you need to design learning for your audience.

WHAT DO YOUR LEARNERS WANT?

Highly motivated learners will learn regardless of the quality of the learning experience. Similarly, unmotivated learners are a challenge even for the best teachers. But the more you can consider your learners' attitudes and motivations, the better you can tailor the learning experience.

You want to consider the question of what your learners want from a few different angles. Think about why they are there, what they want to get out of the experience, what they *don't* want, and what they like (which may be different from what they want).

WHY ARE THEY THERE?

In considering the "why are they there?" questions, let's take a look at some of the types of learners you might encounter:

Would be happy with a list of what to do and a quick run through

On a schedule

Really not interested in your story about that one time with the pineapple...

"Tap tap"

The "Just tell me what I need to know" learner

Hey! Check this out!

Brings lots of motivation to the table

Rampant curiosity

Is actually interested in your story about that one time with the pineapple...

The "Hey! This is cool!" learner

Highly motivated—really highly motivated

Not interested in the backstory

plumbing for dummies

A trial-and-error learner

The "I need to solve a problem" learner

May need to be convinced that the material is useful

Someone for whom the material may not actually be useful

Motivated by other factors like grades or completion

The "This is a required course" learner

Wired for distractions

Short, distributed attention

Thinks they multi-task, but really just switch focus a lot

MAG

The "Oooh, shiny!" learner

That's not the way we've always done it...

Needs to be convinced that the change will be doable and useful

That sounds hard...

Needs time to acclimate and safe opportunities to practice

The "I fear change" learner

Uh huh, uh huh, uh uh, uh huh... oh wait, that's new! uh huh...

Really, really doesn't want to sit through the beginner material (really)

Doesn't need the whole backstory

Understands quickly and gets a lot of the subtleties

The "I pretty much know all of this already" learner

Which type are you? All of the above, most likely—depending on the subject matter and context. You've probably been all of these types at one time or another. You might have been a "required course" learner in math and a "hey, cool!" learner in music (or vice versa).

Ultimately, we are all the "What can I get from this?" learner. We want to know why a learning experience is useful or interesting to us. Regardless of type, people want to have purpose and be able to *do* something with what they are learning.

INTRINSIC VS. EXTRINSIC MOTIVATION

Let's take a look at two people who are learning to program in Java. Pat is an **intrinsically** motivated learner, whereas Chris is **extrinsically** motivated.

Intrinsically motivated learners are interested in the topic for its own sake, or have a specific problem they are trying to solve. Pat wants to use Java to *do* something specific.

Extrinsically motivated learners are motivated by an outside reward or punishment. Any kind of learning that is "required" is likely to be extrinsically motivated. Chris's reasons for learning Java are very different.

As you might imagine, intrinsic motivation kicks extrinsic motivation's ass.

We know that any one person can be a different kind of learner, depending on the subject matter and context. In the same way, a learner's motivation can be intrinsic or extrinsic depending on the circumstances. For example, someone's motivation during the annual sexual harassment prevention seminar may be pretty extrinsic (it's required) but may become a lot more intrinsic later (when an employee comes to them with a sexual harassment complaint).

NOT ALL EXTRINSIC MOTIVATION IS CREATED EQUAL

Self-determination theory, conceived by the researchers Edward Deci and Richard Ryan, is probably the dominant model for motivation right now.

They talk about a continuum of motivation:

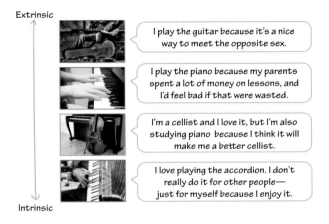

By their definitions, only the final motivation is intrinsic. Deci and Ryan associate intrinsic motivation with activities that are worth doing for their own sakes— things that are enjoyable or satisfying, even if there are no other people involved.

At the opposite end of the spectrum, fully extrinsic motivation is entirely external. People are only seeking a reward or avoiding a punishment.

In between, they list extrinsic reasons that have to do with our sense of social relatedness. This is when you do something because it will please other people, makes you feel part of a group, or supports your sense of identity.

Motivation is rarely all based on a single attribute, but is usually a combination of different variables. For example, I try to keep up with as much educational psychology research as I can, but when I first started trying to read research papers, I realized that my knowledge of research statistics wasn't very strong.

I've since become more knowledgeable about statistics, but not because I have an intrinsic interest in statistics. I've done it because it's necessary for me to feel like a competent professional and because I don't want to make embarrassing mistakes when I interpret data.

Fully external motivation often takes the form of either bribery or compulsion, and is therefore the least effective and durable form of motivation. As soon as the reward or punishment stops, so does the behavior, and people often resent being bribed or compelled, which can destroy any intrinsic motivation they might have had.

HOW DO YOU DEAL WITH EACH TYPE?

Depending on what type of learners you have, there are strategies that you can use to improve the learning experience.

Design strategies for teaching intrinsically motivated learners include:

- **Saying "Thank you" to the learning gods.** Seriously, your life is going to be much easier.
- **Making sure your learners have time to work on their own problems.** You may have some standard activities or challenges that everyone needs to do, but you will get a lot better mileage if learners are working on problems that are meaningful to them.

- **Leveraging your learners as teachers.** Intrinsically motivated learners are going to learn a lot on their own, and will learn even more if they share that knowledge. As they do so, it will expose other students to a wider variety of possible applications. It also takes the pressure off you to be the only source of information and energy, which means both you and your learners win.

Design strategies for teaching extrinsically motivated learners include:

- **Scouring their situation for intrinsic motivators.** Is there anything— *anything*—that they find intrinsically motivating about the subject matter? Ask lots of questions about what they might do with the information. Try to tie it back to relevant, real-world tasks or to their sense of identity as professionals.
- **Having them tell you.** Start with your learners telling you why a topic is useful or important. If you tell them, they may be resistant or skeptical, but if they come up with the reasons, they are likely to at least be a little more receptive.
- **Looking for pain points.** If your learners are unfamiliar with the material, they won't be able to make connections between their aggravations and the solutions you are offering, but if you can figure out what annoys them and show them how they can alleviate that annoyance, you can transform extrinsic into intrinsic in moments.
- **Avoiding extensive theory and background.** You may find that academic stuff fascinating, but extrinsically motivated learners would rather stab themselves in the eye with the free pen. Stick with specific examples and challenges that directly relate to real-life scenarios. In fact, this is usually true for *all* learners. If you've got a lot of backstory, and you can't say exactly why it's important, then you should cut it. Seriously—highlight and delete (or at least move it to the appendix or the resource section).
- **Using interesting hypothetical problems to awaken their intrinsic motivation.** If you start with a genuinely interesting challenge or puzzle that the learner needs to solve, their extrinsic motivation will start to drift toward a more intrinsic motivation, like puzzle-solving or accomplishing the challenge. Just keep in mind that when I say "interesting" I mean "interesting to them."

SCENARIO: INTRODUCING DRY MATERIAL

Here's an example of a design challenge for extrinsically motivated learners. Several years ago, I was looking at an elearning course designed for high school students to take online. The courses had lovely, flashy graphics and animation. I opened the first course, which was on statistics, and the first thing that happened was a very enthusiastic announcer saying, "Welcome to this course. Let's start with the....History...Of...Statistics!!"

How many high school students do you think are going to be intrinsically motivated by the history of statistics?

Yeah, not so much. In fact, it's safe to say that without the extrinsic rewards and punishments, they wouldn't be anywhere near this topic.

If you want to get a little intrinsic motivation from this bunch, how could you introduce the topic differently?

—TAKE A MOMENT TO CONSIDER WHAT YOU WOULD DO BEFORE MOVING ON—

Some possible ideas include:

- Use famous or controversial statistics (e.g., "50 percent of all marriages end in divorce") and have students research what those numbers really mean and how they are derived.
- Look at statistics that impact their lives (census data, school funding, etc.).
- Make it about money (that's always interesting).
- Have them decide which used car to buy based on statistical data. ■

YOUR LEARNERS WANT TO NOT FEEL STUPID

A few times over the years I've had this conversation with clients:

CLIENT: We want to do a basic overview for people. Essentially, we want to do "Our Topic for Dummies." But we can't say "dummies," of course. We can't suggest that people are dumb.

ME: I don't think people take it that way.

CLIENT: Regardless, we'll have to call it something else.

It's an interesting question, right? Why would anyone buy a book for "dummies"? Clearly, people do buy them, and it's probably not because they think they aren't smart.

I've always argued that the whole point of the dummy/complete idiot's/beginner's books is that instead of calling you dumb, their main selling point is that they promise *not* to make you feel stupid.

If I pick up a guide to wine that assumes I know the difference between a cabernet and a merlot, then I'm already feeling a little sheepish about my own ignorance. But suppose I pick up a book that doesn't assume I know the difference between Riesling and tap water. In this case, when I do know something, I can feel superior without risk.

A friend of mine is a game designer who is now designing elearning programs. When he talks about game design, he says, "My job as a game designer is to make the player feel smart." I think the same is true for learning designers. Your job is to make your learners feel smart, and, even more importantly, they should feel capable.

The "I don't want to feel stupid" learner

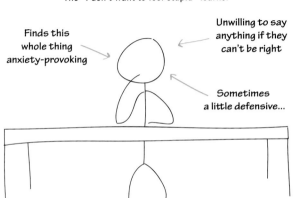

It's fine to challenge your learners—this isn't about making it easy for them. Things that are too easy can feel tedious and unsatisfying for learners. But you don't want to have your learners feel shame about what they do and don't know. Instead, you want to give your learners a safe path into the material.

Dan Meyer, a math teacher and blogger (http://blog.mrmeyer.com), describes the process he uses when introducing a problem to students:

> We take guesses—What do you think? What do you know is a wrong answer? I'll ask a struggling learner for a wrong answer. Give me a number that's too high. Give me a number that's too low. I'm involving students at a very low investment that has a huge return.

Some ways to engage wary learners:

- **Leverage what they already know.** Can you take advantage of any knowledge they already have about the topic?
- **Give them some early success.** What can be something they can achieve early on? Is there some accomplishment that they can tackle with the material within the first lesson?
- **Give them some control.** Wary learners may feel like the learning experience is something they don't have any control over, so giving some control—for example, the ability to decide the order or pace of material—may help them feel more a part of the process.
- **Create safe places to fail.** Can they practice or self-assess in a private or non-judgmental environment?

If you do this well, then when they do start to succeed, your learners will feel like they *own* the subject matter. If you pull that off, then *you* win as the learning designer.

WHAT DO YOUR LEARNERS LIKE?

In addition to knowing what your learners want, you also want to ask what they like. My game-designer friend advocates finding out about your learners' preferences:

> ...You can see that if we are going to focus on developing software that our users want and like, it's essential that we know and understand our audience, not just the subject matter.

I would suggest that you research the brands, hobbies, and media (television, films, games, websites, etc.) that your target audience enjoys. This should give you a better idea of the aesthetics and interactions that your learners like and want. (Raymer 2011)

If you think about it, this makes perfect sense. If your audience loves basketball or knitting or opera or reality television, why wouldn't you want to utilize that to make your learning design more engaging for your learners? Obviously, your entire audience won't like exactly the same TV shows, but if you can find a common thread, you can use that in your design.

WHAT IS THEIR CURRENT SKILL LEVEL?

One of the things you need to consider when you are finding out about your learners is their current skill level. Basically, you want to know how steep the climb is going to be for them.

Are you asking your learners to do this?

Or this?

And how much of an effort are you asking your learners to make?

This question is complicated by the fact that while you have some control over the difficulty of the material, much of the outcome is determined not by your design but by the learners' ability.

For example, you may be building something that seems—to you—to function at a fairly reasonable level of effort.

But to a complete novice, it feels pretty steep.

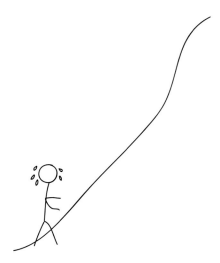

If someone is already an expert, then the material may require no effort at all.

The difficulty of a learning experience is actually a derived value based not only on the complexity of the content but also on the prior knowledge of the learner:

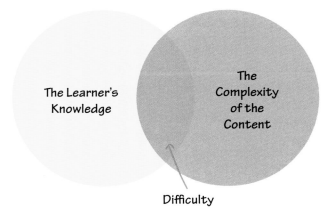

Difficulty

Let's say you're working with a novice jogger, a pretty good amateur runner, and an experienced professional marathoner. Each person would not only need a different *level* of instruction, but actually would need very different approaches.

For a novice jogger, the learning experience you need to provide would include:

- Lots of guidance
- A careful introduction that doesn't go too quickly in the beginning
- A structured experience that has immediate, achievable goals
- Strategies for increasing self-confidence
- A gradual progression of difficulty, with opportunities to rest
- Coaching and feedback on how they are doing

For a proficient recreational runner, you would include:

- Some practice of new concepts
- Advanced topic information
- Coaching and shaping for improvement of existing behaviors
- Much more autonomy

The expert marathoner would want:

- Somebody to hold out the bananas and water and then get the hell out of the way
- Really expert coaching
- Information about specific challenges (e.g., the characteristics of a particular route)
- Some help with measuring progress (mile marking, timekeeping, etc.)
- Full autonomy
- The opportunity to act as a resource by teaching or coaching others

Aside from the bananas, these characteristics hold true for almost any discipline. A more beginner audience needs a lot of structure and guidance, and a more advanced audience needs more autonomy and resources that they can choose to access as needed.

SOME LEARNERS ALREADY KNOW A LOT

We've already looked at the idea that the same content can look pretty steep to a novice but be more like this for an expert:

People are faster on the straightaways.

If somebody is already an expert, they can pretty much zoom along until they come to a gap in their knowledge or hit an unusual or novel concept or dilemma. Then they need to slow down and absorb the needed information or skill, and then they can be off and running again.

Unfortunately, a single learning design is frequently expected to accommodate many different levels of learners.

This means that all the things you built into the learner's journey to support novices (careful guidance, lots of practice, slowly helping them build their mental model before adding in content) are pretty much guaranteed to make the expert absolutely *nuts*.

This is the equivalent of being the experienced flyer standing in the TSA security line with your laptop out, liquids in a bag, shoes off, and carry-on ready to go, trapped behind what appears to be a grandma who hasn't flown since 1972 and an entire daycare of small children with all their associated paraphernalia.

Whole spectrums of learners frequently get shoved through the same learning experience for reasons of budget or convenience.

If that has to be the case, consider the following suggestions:

- **Don't make them hate you.** Don't make every part of the learning experience required for everybody. Just don't. Really. This means don't make people sit through classroom training they don't need—make parts of the classroom experience optional or take-home. This also means that you shouldn't lock down a menu in an elearning environment, forcing people to go through it in order or require them to wait until the entire audio narration has played before you let them advance to the next screen.
- **Consider pull versus push**. Novice learners frequently don't know what they don't know, but experts frequently have a pretty good idea. You can generally trust experts to get the information they need if you make sure that it's easily available and applicable.
  Pull means you provide the resources, lessons, and reference materials and the learners choose when they need them. You want to make them as easy to find and as accessible as possible, but you don't need to force them through it.
- **Leverage their expertise.** These are smart people! Figure out ways to make use of that. Can they coach novices? Can they have special access to the course to add their own experiences and stories to make the course more vivid for novices? If you can figure out a way for them to use their expertise to enhance the journey for others (and learn a few things along the way), then they will have a whole different level of engagement with the material.
- **Embed some of the novice information.** If, for example, you're providing vocabulary for the more novice learners in an elearning program, make that vocabulary available by rolling over the word rather than spelling it out in the main content. That way, it's there if your novice needs it, but it doesn't slow down the more knowledgeable learners.
- **Let them test out (maybe).** One of the most common tactics for addressing varying difficulty levels is to say, "We'll have a pre-test! So if people really know the information, they don't have to take the course!" Here's the thing with this. This is a perfectly reasonable approach *if* you think you can create

a genuinely effective pre-test that measures knowledge or skill. Honestly, I've not seen that many good pre-tests. They tend to be either trivia questions or so easy that any reasonably astute person could guess their way through to a passing score. It's *hard* to write a good assessment. And if you are trying to assess a *skill*—something that had to be developed over time and through practice—well, how likely are you to be able to do that with something like a multiple-choice quiz?

Skills can be assessed, but they usually need to be assessed through observation of competencies rather than multiple-choice tests (unless the competency you are assessing is the ability to take tests). One elearning professional I met at a conference has devised a method to evaluate the pre-test: He has a student who knows nothing about the content take the test. If they score above 40%, he knows that the test isn't really assessing the material.

- **Ask "Do you need anything?" and then get out of their way.** If you are supporting an expert marathoner, you don't say, "Hey, let's wait for some of the newer folks to catch up" or "Have you seen this brochure on ways to motivate your training regimen?" Instead, you say, "Need anything? Banana? Water? No? OK—see you at the next mile marker then!" The same goes for learning resources: Figure out what they need, make sure they have access, and then stop bothering them.

SCAFFOLD THE INCLINE

What if the topic is too complicated for novice learners to really tackle without hopelessly oversimplifying the content? What if putting the content into a realistic context means that context is overwhelming to the user? Try scaffolding.

SCAFFOLDING: Build supports to make the learning incline less steep. Then gradually reduce those supports until learners can handle the incline on their own.

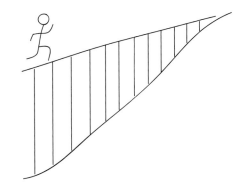

Good scaffolding acts like training wheels; it allows learners to accomplish the difficult task in a safely supported way. Ideally, it doesn't reduce learners to bystanders but gives them the support they need to complete tasks they wouldn't otherwise be able to do.

Examples of ways to scaffold:

- **Reduce the complexity of the environment.** Let's say you want to use an elearning simulation to teach someone about the controls in a plane cockpit, but it's too overwhelming for a novice learner. To scaffold their learning experience, you could fade out all but a few of the key controls for the first few scenarios, and then gradually add controls back in as the learner becomes more proficient and competent.
- **Use walkthroughs.** Have the learner go through the whole process with a simplified case. For example, if you want to teach students about the scientific research process, have them work through a very simple research problem with step-by-step guidance and pretty obvious results, and then move on to more complex cases.

  Another example: I once created a fairly complicated environment for salespeople to learn a specific sales process by selling technical products to several virtual customers. Their very first scenario was a short and slightly silly example where they sold snowsuits in Hawaii, which gave them the opportunity to learn the interface and the sales process without worrying about the technical content right away.
- **Provide supports.** If possible, embed easily accessed references in the experience. For example, have samples, definitions, or help documentation right at hand so the learners can have the support they need while in the midst of trying to accomplish the task.

HOW ARE YOUR LEARNERS DIFFERENT FROM YOU?

The first thing you need to know is:

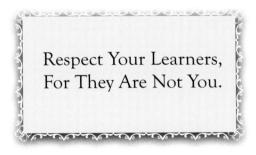

Respect Your Learners, For They Are Not You.

Seriously, I'm getting this made up as a bumper sticker. It's one of the most important things you can remember.

Let me give you an example. Several years ago I was reading an article about different work styles, and the article categorized people into four broad types, with questions to help you identify your own type.

I was reading the description of my type and nodding a fair bit. My type enjoys problem-solving? Absolutely. Yep, I like new challenges. Yes, the opportunity to learn new things *was* a good motivational reward for me.

And then I stopped.

And I looked at the other three types, while one of those cartoon light bulbs was going off over my head. I love learning new things (it's how I wound up in instructional design), *but not everybody feels the same way.*

This should not have been news to me, but it was. You mean there are people who are mostly comfortable with the safe and familiar? People for whom learning something new is scary or uncomfortable? Or people who primarily regard it as a nuisance, or a necessary evil to be dispensed with or circumvented as quickly possible? Really?

Whoa.

I was seriously ashamed of myself—I had been subconsciously assuming that my experience was the norm. Quite possibly you've never shared that particular blind spot, but everyone inevitably thinks about teaching through the filter of their own experience. What learning experiences were effective for you? How do you like to learn? Surely other people would also like to learn in similar ways, right?

That's mostly right, actually, but it's important to keep in mind that not everybody will have the same focus and motivation. Also, your learner does not see the world the same way you do.

WHAT IS YOUR LEARNER'S CONTEXT?

Consider your learner's context for the material.

You have a lot of context for the material you know, and your learners frequently have quite a bit less context.

Read the following paragraph:

> First, you will need to provide support above the usual level. If you do not have a device for this elevation, you will need to obtain one. Before you provide the elevation support, you will want to decrease the later resistance for all the critical contact points. After the elevation device has been utilized, you can complete the rotation of the critical contact points, and exchange the impacted element. You will then want to re-engage the critical contact points and remove the device. You may continue to use the replacement element. If it is not adequate for long-term use, you may want to repair or replace the original element, at which point you will need to repeat the process.

Was it difficult to follow? Did you have to force yourself to concentrate to understand or process what was being said?

OK, now try this version. Take a look at this picture and then read the paragraph again.

> First, you will need to provide support above the usual level. If you do not have a device for this elevation, you will need to obtain one. Before you provide the elevation support, you will want to decrease the later resistance for all the critical contact points. After the elevation device has been utilized, you can complete the rotation of the critical contact points, and exchange the impacted element. You will then want to re-engage the critical contact points and remove the device. You may continue to use the replacement element. If it is not adequate for long-term use, you may want to repair or replace the original element, at which point you will need to repeat the process.

Did it make more sense the second time around?

The tire-changing example was based on an experiment (Bransford 1972). They also used a similar example where the task was doing laundry, and they had three groups:

- A group that was told it was laundry before they read the paragraph
- A group that was not told the example referred to laundry
- A group that was told that it was laundry only after they'd read the paragraph

Unsurprisingly, the group that understood and remembered the most was the group that knew what the example was about before they read the paragraph. They were able to understand and retain the information specifically because they already had a mental picture about laundry that they were able to use to parse the information.

This is important to keep in mind because whenever you have a lot of knowledge about something, you have a picture in your mind, and your learners may not.

HOW MUCH YOU KNOW VS. HOW MUCH THEY KNOW

Let's say you are teaching an introductory course on something you know a lot about. But of course you can't talk to a novice audience the same way you'd talk to a colleague. So what's the bigger barrier? Is it how much they know (not much)? Or is it how much *you* know (a lot)?

Well, sometimes the barrier genuinely is how little your learner knows:

But just as often the barrier is how much you know and—more importantly—how hard it is for you to remember what it was like *not* to know it. Have you ever had somebody explain something technical or complicated and just not been able to follow what they were telling you? If so, you know that you don't want your learners to experience that.

It can sometimes be hard to avoid, because of the way we mentally organize information.

WHY YOUR BRAIN IS LIKE A CLOSET

Think about a subject in which you have expertise. What kind of mental model do you have?

Is your understanding and organization of the subject like this?

Or is it more like this?

If you are the expert, it's likely that you have the first kind of mental model—pretty orderly, with a lot of different categories, distinctions, and a sophisticated way of organizing the information. If you are the novice, you have a lot less structure around your limited information.

If somebody hands an expert a blue sweater to put in the closet, that expert will be able to decide pretty quickly where to put that sweater because they already have a structure in place (on the sweater shelf, next to other winter clothing, ordered by weight or style or even color).

But when you hand content to a novice learner, that person is likely to look perplexedly at the piece of information that they have no context for, shrug, and toss it onto the pile of other information accumulating on the floor of their closet. We've all had those training experiences where you get a flood of information and all you can do is try to keep up.

The bigger problem comes when you want someone to *retrieve* the information. As the expert, you have all sorts of ways to pull out a particular piece of information—you can check sweaters, check winter clothing, check casual wear, or check things that are blue. At the same time, your learner is pawing randomly through their pile, with no other strategy than to try really hard to remember.

HOW DO YOU HELP NOVICES STRUCTURE THEIR CLOSETS?

The first thing you need to do is help your learners build a few shelves.

There's no way that any single class or training program is going to get them all the way to your mental model, and you shouldn't try (that's just as bad as burying them under a flood of multi-colored laundry). But you can definitely provide some context for the information that you are going to give them.

Here are a few ways to help your learners build shelves:

Use a high-level organizer. Start them with some structure that will help them organize what follows. This could be a road map of the broad categories, an overview of the basic principles, or an acronym or a mnemonic device. This gives them some shelves on which to start putting information.

Use visuals. Visual information contains several extra cues that give your learner more hooks for storing and retrieving the information.

Use a story. People have amazingly sticky memories for well-told stories, particularly ones that arouse emotions.

Work through problems. One way experts categorize information is by how they can use it to solve a problem (that is, how they can apply it). Working through problems helps novices start developing their own similar structure.

Have learners design shelves. Give learners the information as a specific task, and have them decide how it should be organized. Ask them how they would present it if they had to teach it to others. You can then have them compare their organization to the expert view and let them think about what they would do differently in the future.

Use a metaphor or an analogy. Compare the relevant subject matter to something that your learners are already familiar with so that you can leverage the storage and retrieval capability of one of their existing mental models. It's frequently a good idea to use something common and everyday that the learner can't help but be familiar with, like, oh, say—a closet.

It's worth mentioning that although it's more common to have experts teaching novice learners, that's not always the case. Sometimes experts teach other experts, or, most difficult, an expert is teaching an audience of widely mixed levels of expertise.

As mentioned, people who already have a lot of expertise really don't need a lot of setup—they know where the blue sweater goes and just want to get on with it.

Learning experiences for people who already have a lot of expertise should be efficient and should be more "pull" than "push." Let them decide when they need it and how much.

Whenever possible, you want to make sure that a knowledgeable person has a fast-forward lane, so they can get the necessary information without having to wade through all the material they already know.

THE EXPERIENCE FILTER

All learners, both novice and expert, filter their new learning through their past experience. Humans are sense-making animals. We will try to interpret and make explanations for things we don't understand.

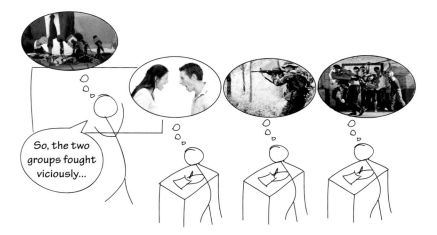

This is OK, and a perfectly normal part of learning. Everyone's understanding is colored by previous experience, and therefore everybody's understanding of the same material will be a bit different.

Sometimes, though, that can lead to critical misconceptions, as here:

> **BARISTA-IN-TRAINING:** This customer wants one of the St. Patrick's Day Peppermint Wasabi Double Espressos, and he's paying with a credit card. I haven't done a credit card yet.
>
> **EXPERIENCED BARISTA:** (thinks "OK, he's the first one today to order that disgusting seasonal specialty") OK, mark it as a specialty order, and I'll show you how to run the credit card.

Hours later...

> **EXPERIENCED BARISTA:** (checking receipts) What the hell? 107 specialty orders? Is that right?
>
> **BARISTA-IN-TRAINING:** I think so—a lot of people paid with credit cards today.

HOW CAN YOU KNOW WHAT YOUR LEARNERS ARE THINKING?

Unless you can read minds, you need to make sure the information flows both ways.

The traditional lecture classroom is probably the most common, familiar model that people recognize for how learning works: The teacher pours information into the heads of learners.

The problem with this is that the information is flowing in only one direction.

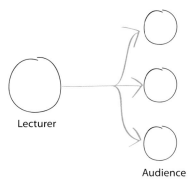

A lecturer could talk for days and not have any idea what misconceptions his or her students might have. Eventually, in traditional classrooms, misconceptions may turn up on an assignment, but only long after the information has settled into the learner's mind and the ideal opportunity to correct the misconception has passed.

A better model is an interactive one that has information flowing in both directions:

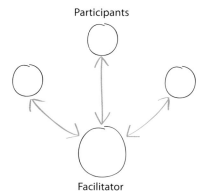

Regardless of the learning venue (classroom, elearning, informational website), it's best to have as interactive an experience as possible. Ideally, you would construct opportunities to see how your learners are interpreting and applying what they learn, so you can correct misconceptions, extend their understanding, and identify ways to reinforce the learning.

LEARNING STYLES

But wait, what about the "I'm an auditory, visual, tactile, kinesthetic, conceptual, social" learner? Don't we also want to know our audience's learning styles?

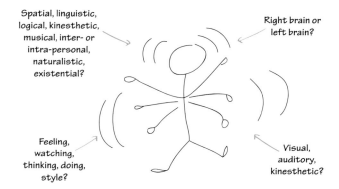

Maybe you are familiar with the concept of learning styles. For example, you've probably heard of someone being described as a "visual learner."

Basically, the idea espoused by learning-style advocates was that if we could identify individual differences in how people learn, we could provide them with learning experiences that best match their learning styles and improve learning outcomes.

There are many intelligence- or learning-style inventories. Here are a few of the more prominent ones:

- Gardner's Multiple Intelligences—Howard Gardner proposes that people have different kinds of intelligences (spatial, linguistic, logical, kinesthetic, musical, interpersonal, intrapersonal, naturalistic, and existential) rather than a single type of IQ (intelligence quotient).
- VAK or VARK—This model proposes that people have inclinations toward learning styles, such as visual, auditory, reading, or kinesthetic learning.
- Kolb's Learning Styles Inventory—David A. Kolb proposes a set of learning styles (converger, diverger, assimilator, and accommodator) based on preferences for abstract versus concrete and active versus reflective learning.

WHAT CAN I DO WITH LEARNING STYLES?

Not much. Sorry, but the scientific evidence of effective use of learning styles is pretty weak (at the time of the writing of this book). There are a couple of assumptions that can't really be proved: first, that somebody's learning style can easily be measured, and second, that there is a practical way to adapt the learning experience to those styles. Technology may solve this problem eventually, but for now we don't really have effective examples of this.

I bring this up because learning styles are pretty popular, but they haven't proven to be very effective. That may change in the future as people investigate better ways to assess and apply learning styles.

Still, all is not lost; there are some useful ideas you *can* get from the learning styles conversation:

- **Not everyone learns the same way.** Even if you can't adapt a learning situation to someone's unique learning style, you can create learning experiences that incorporate a variety of approaches. This also helps keep a learning experience interesting and provides a variety of memory triggers. Varying the learning styles also battles against people's tendency toward habituation (more on this later).
- **There are different kinds of intelligence.** I used to teach art students, and they loved learning about multiple intelligences because it validated their skills and abilities that fell outside the traditional definition of IQ.
- **We are more alike than we are different.** Excepting certain physical impairments, we all learn from visual, auditory, and kinesthetic methods, and we have all the different types of intelligence at varying levels.
- **You may want to vary the learning approach depending on the subject being learned.** Although there is little evidence to support customizing learning to a particular learner's style, there is some evidence that suggests that you should adapt the learning approach to the content being taught. At a minimum, use common sense to match the approach to the task. You wouldn't want your car mechanic trained via audiobook, right?

METHODS FOR LEARNING ABOUT YOUR LEARNERS

So how do you find out about your learners? There are several good books on the topic of analysis for instructional design (start with Allison Rossett's *First Things Fast*), and there's a lot to be learned from the field of user experience about how to research your audience.

I'm not going to get into a lot of detail about this, but here are a few key practices that I believe are crucial for good audience analysis:

* Talk to your learners
* Follow your learners around
* Try stuff out with your learners

TALK TO YOUR LEARNERS

This may sound unbelievably obvious, but in my experience, a lot of learning gets designed without talking to learners. As an instructional designer, I've had a number of projects where I talk to project stakeholders, to trainers, to managers, and to subject matter experts. Unless I insist on it, I rarely get to talk to the actual learners. To be fair, most of these experts have a lot of experience with the subject matter and with the learners, so they are great sources of information, but they also have pretty sophisticated closets. You should talk to all of those people *and* you should talk to your learners.

Here are a few reasons why:

* **They will tell you how it works, not how it should work.** Stakeholders, managers, and experts are often very vested in the "right" way to do something. They'll tell you how the manual says to do it, but your learners will frequently tell you what happens in the real world. In theory, loan-closing requests are scheduled "by the book," but actually the customer service people use a particular shortcut. In theory, programmers write their own subroutine for a particular function, but really everyone goes to the same open-source code site and copies the free code that's posted there. You may still need to teach the official version, but you can create better scenarios and support materials if you know how it really happens.
* **They can tell you where it hurts.** Your best friend when designing learning is someone who is currently learning the topic or has just recently learned it. They are very clear on what was confusing or difficult. They can tell you what made sense to them, what was easy, and what they are still struggling with.
* **They can give you examples and context.** Learners' comments, complaints, suggestions, and ideas can give you all the little details necessary to create really good learning scenarios. Your experts can sometimes do this as well, but sometimes their examples get a little out of date, whereas your current learners frequently know what the current challenges are.

Some questions you should ask learners:

- Why are you learning this?
- How will learning this help you (how are they motivated)?
- What are the biggest hassles or challenges you experience (in relation to the topic)?
- What are some examples of when you've had problems?
- What was the hardest thing for you to learn?
- What were the easy parts?
- What could make it easier for you?
- How do you use this information now?
- What do you wish you had known when you first started?
- Can you walk me through it?
- What does a typical example look like?
- What crazy exceptions have you seen?

FOLLOW YOUR LEARNERS AROUND

Sometimes this important process is called job shadowing, and in the user experience community it's often referred to as contextual inquiry, but it basically amounts to following your learners around in their actual environment.

This is not focus groups, email surveys, or phone interviews. This is face-to-face in the environment where they will be using the learning. Could be an office, a factory, their computer setup in their den—wherever. If you can do only one type of audience analysis, do this (you can always ask your questions along the way).

Why is following your learners around important?

- **Context, context, context.** You want your learning to create contextual triggers that will allow learners to remember things later. We'll talk more about this in Chapter 4, but people remember more in a similar environment than they do in a dissimilar environment, and the more context (visual or situational) that you can leverage, the better people will remember.
- **Even new learners have started to build some shelves.** Even if you are talking to new learners, they've already started to develop their closets, which means that they've probably already automated some of the steps in their brains. If you're asking them about what they do, they are already starting to gloss over details, but if you watch them in their actual environments, you see what's happening and can stop and get more information; for example, "Can you tell me more about that step you just did?"

- **Juicy details.** If you are trying to create good examples or scenarios for learning, you can get the best details from seeing people in their actual environments. If you know about their world, you can much more easily create better examples, scenarios, and activities.

TRY STUFF OUT WITH YOUR LEARNERS

Frequently, analysis gets done, and then the learning designer goes away and designs the learning and it gets distributed to the learners. If someone is teaching face to face, they get a decent amount of feedback in the process of teaching the class. If the learning is delivered by other people, or if it is elearning, sometimes very little feedback reaches the learning designer.

Try stuff out with your learners along the way. If you have an idea for an activity, get a few people to try it out. Create prototypes, do user testing, run pilot tests.

This is not the same thing as showing it to someone and getting their feedback. Getting people to review your materials can be useful, but everyone fills in the gaps with their own understanding. Nothing will show up gaps like trying stuff out. Have a quick and dirty test of a lesson or an activity. Watch users try an elearning program. Do a pilot of a class with a small sympathetic audience.

Are there parts where people get confused? Do certain parts drag? Do you find yourself talking for a long time in the middle? Was your test audience confused by the instructions for an activity? Testing your learning design early and often will allow you to fix these things before you get in front of your official learners. All the learning theory in the world won't help you as much as testing your learning designs and fixing the problems.

There are a few reasons why this is important:

- **You think you are being clear, but you *know* how it's supposed to work.** Anyone who designs anything gets a certain amount of tunnel vision. If you try things out, you can find out what does and doesn't make sense to a learner before you've invested too much time and effort into what might be a wrong direction.
- **You'll get good ideas.** You'll think of all sorts of good ways to refine the design that you could never have come up with in a vacuum.
- **It's more efficient in the end.** If you regularly try things out, you can do lean versions and just fill in where there are issues. This means you can create much shorter, more efficient lessons than if you try to guess what your audience knows.

SUMMARY

- You want to know about your learners—not just about their demographics, but about their motivation, likes and dislikes, skill level, and ways of understanding the world.
- Provide more structure for your new learners, and more resources and autonomy for your experienced learners.
- Don't just hand your learners information, but instead help them construct and organize their framework for that information.
- Learning experiences should be two-way interactions, so you know when learners understand correctly and when they don't.
- All of the theory in the world won't help you as much as spending time in your learners' world, and testing your designs early and often.

REFERENCES

Bransford, J.D. and M. K. Johnson. 1972. "Contextual Prerequisites for Understanding: Some Investigations of Comprehension and Recall." *Journal of Verbal Learning and Verbal Behavior* 11: 717–726.

Chi, M. T. H., P. Feltovich, and R. Glaser. 1981. "Categorization and Representation of Physics Problems by Experts and Novices." *Cognitive Science* 5: 121–152.

Coffield, F., D. Moseley, E. Hall, and K. Ecclestone. 2004. *Learning Styles and Pedagogy in Post-16 Learning: A Systematic and Critical Review.* London: Learning and Skills Research Centre.

Deci, E. L., and R. M. Ryan. 1985. *Intrinsic Motivation and Self-Determination in Human Behavior.* New York: Plenum.

Fleming, N.D. and C. Mills. 1992. "Not Another Inventory, Rather a Catalyst for Reflection." *To Improve the Academy* 11: 137.

Gardner, Howard. *1999. Intelligence Reframed: Multiple Intelligences for the 21st Century.* New York: Basic Books.

Kolb., David A. and R. Fry. 1975. "Toward an Applied Theory of Experiential Learning." *Theories of Group Process,* C. Copper (ed.). London: John Wiley.

Meyer, Dan. YouTube video on real-world math, www.youtube.com/watch?v=jRMVjHjYB6w.

Paschler, H., M. McDaniel, D. Rohrer, and R. Bjork. 2010. "Learning Styles: Concepts and Evidence." *Psychological Science in the Public Interest* 9: 105–119.

Raymer, R. 2011. "Gamification: Using Game Mechanics to Enhance Elearning." *eLearn Magazine* (http://elearnmag.acm.org), in review.

WHAT'S THE GOAL?

DETERMINE GOALS

Whenever you are designing a learning experience, it's critical to have clear goals defined. If you don't know where you are and where your learners need to be, you can't figure out how to get them there.

If you don't have a clear destination, you can't plot a clear path and you certainly can't communicate that path to your learner:

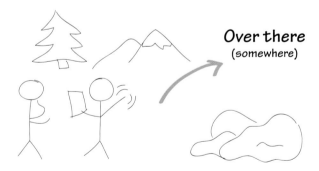

Over there
(somewhere)

In determining the path for your learner, you want to do these things:

- Identify what problem you are trying to solve.
- Set a destination.
- Determine the gaps between the starting point and the destination.
- Decide how far you are going to be able to go.

IDENTIFY THE PROBLEM

In the first chapter we talked about identifying the gaps. You want to start with the gaps when identifying the destination.

UH HUH, AND *WHY* DO THEY NEED KNOW THAT?

I've had some variant of this conversation with clients many times over the years:

CLIENT:	The salespeople just need to understand the basics of insurance underwriting/cellular service/ cloud computing. That's the learning objective.
LEARNING DESIGNER:	OK, sure, and why is it important they know that?
CLIENT:	Well, they just need to be grounded in the basics.
LEARNING DESIGNER:	Uh huh. And what will they actually do with that information?
CLIENT:	They just need to know it.
LEARNING DESIGNER:	And what bad thing could happen if they don't know it?
CLIENT:	Well, they'd look stupid in front of clients.
LEARNING DESIGNER:	Ah! Great. So maybe the learning objective is something more like "Salespeople should be able to answer customer questions accurately."
CLIENT:	Yeah, I guess that makes sense.

Before you start designing a learning experience, you need to know what problem you are trying to solve.

A lot of learning projects start with the goal rather than the problem, but that puts you in the position of solving problems you don't actually have, while failing to address the real issues.

For example, let's look at this goal and some possible solutions:

Goal	Possible Solutions
Marianna will be able to give appropriate and timely feedback to her staff.	Marianna could watch another supervisor model good feedback.
	Marianna could take an elearning course on coaching and providing feedback for employees.
	Marianna could role-play feedback scenarios with other staff members.

All of those solutions could potentially address the stated goal. Let's take a look at the same set of choices with the gap identified first.

Gap	Goal	Possible Solutions
Marianna was recently promoted, and is struggling with giving feedback to people who used to be her peers (skills/ motivation gap).	Marianna will be able to give appropriate and timely feedback to her staff.	Marianna could watch another supervisor model good feedback. Marianna could take an elearning course on coaching and providing feedback for employees. Marianna could role-play feedback scenarios with other staff members.

The goal is still valid, but now some of the possible solutions are better than others—observing other supervisors and role-playing become better solutions than taking a knowledge-based course.

Here's another example:

Goal	Possible Solutions
Members of the repair staff need to be knowledgeable about basic principles of electricity.	Course on introduction to electrical physics Simulation for troubleshooting common electrical problems Lesson on dangers of electricity Simulation lesson on making electrical circuits

Let's take a look at this same one with the gaps:

Gap	Goal	Possible Solutions
Newly hired repair staff members frequently lack the knowledge and skills to troubleshoot customer electrical problems safely.	Repair staff needs to be knowledgeable about basic principles of electricity.	Course on introduction to electrical physics Simulation for troubleshooting common electrical problems Lesson on dangers of electricity Simulation lesson on making electrical circuits

As with the previous example, when we use the gap definition, some of the possible solutions are better than others.

Some questions to ask to help identify the problem:

- "What bad thing will happen if they don't know this?"
- "What are they actually going to do with this information?"
- "How will you know if they are doing it right?"
- "What does it look like if they get it wrong?"
- "So why is it important they know that? Uh huh, and why is *that* important?" (repeat as needed)

BREAK IT DOWN

Sometimes a topic is just too big to be precise:

> Students need to learn to be better managers.

That's like saying, "Meet me in Africa." It's a destination, but it doesn't help you book a flight. In those instances, you want to start breaking it down:

> Students need to schedule restaurant employees so all shifts are adequately covered.

> Students need to provide appropriate feedback to an employee who is chronically late for work.

Once you start breaking these down, you can formulate much more specific routes and destinations to get where you need to go.

SOMETIMES THERE IS NO PROBLEM

Sometimes there really is no problem to be solved.

I might take a class in film appreciation just for my own satisfaction, but I wouldn't expect the learning objectives to make me a professional film critic. A community-education course on Taiwanese cooking, a painting class at a local art museum, or even a high school French class isn't really set up in response to a "problem."

NOT ALL JOURNEYS ARE ABOUT THE DESTINATION: Some are about taking a nice walk somewhere pleasant or about getting in shape. Even when the learning isn't in response to a problem, it's likely to be in response to a need or desire.

What do the learners want or need to get out of the experience? If you are creating learning experiences that are primarily for enrichment, you will still create better experiences if you consider and define those wants or needs.

SET THE DESTINATION

After you've defined the problem, you need to define your goal(s).

The more specific you can be about this, the better you can design the path to get there. For example, let's say someone is teaching a Java programming class and the objective is:

> Students will understand how to program in Java.

This is a learning objective pretty much guaranteed to make a formally trained instructional designer's head explode:

There are actually a number of problems with this learning objective, but let's start with the use of the word *understand*.

It's a totally reasonable place to start—of course we want our learners to understand, but there's no visible way to see if someone "understands." It's hard to design for something as fuzzy as "understand," so we need to define it more.

One way some people get around this is by using "doing" words in their learning objectives:

> Students will be able to explain the value of computation for modeling and simulation.

> Students will be able to describe the proper use of method calls.

> Students will be able to define and describe the use of core data structures such as arrays, linked lists, trees, and stacks.

They use words like *define*, *describe*, and *explain* because those are observable actions—you can witness someone describing, defining, or explaining.

Of course, this is a hedge; it doesn't really get you around the problem, unless you are having people memorize and recite definitions. In fact, it's almost as difficult to determine if they can *define* something as it is to know if they *understand* something. Besides, you don't actually care if they can *define* it—you want to know if they can *do* it.

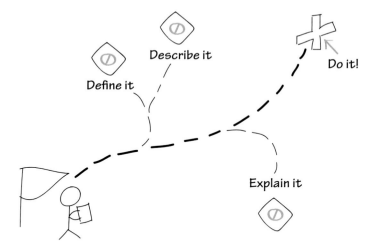

Using those kinds of approximations is basically saying, "I don't know exactly how to explain what I want, but I'm pretty sure this gets them in the neighborhood."

Ultimately, since we care not about what they know but about what they can *do,* the learning objectives should reflect that:

> The student will be able to create a simple, fully functional user interface that collects customer data and transmits that data to the database.

So when you are creating learning objectives, ask yourself:

*   Is this something the learner would actually do in the real world?
*   Can I tell when they've done it?

If the answer to either of those questions is *no,* then you might want to reconsider your learning objective.

Learning Objective	Would Do in Real Life?	Can Tell If They've Done It?
Learner should be able to identify all the criteria necessary to select the correct product for that client.	Yes/No	Yes/No
Learner should be able to list all common Dutch prepositions from memory.	Yes/No	Yes/No
Learner should understand project-management roles and responsibilities.	Yes/No	Yes/No
Learner should be able to create a website that works on the five most common web browsers.	Yes/No	Yes/No
Learner should be able to state the legal definition of sexual harassment.	Yes/No	Yes/No
Learner should be able to identify whether a complaint meets the definition of sexual harassment, and be able to state the reasons why.	Yes/No	Yes/No
Learner will understand the limitations of JavaScript as a programming tool.	Yes/No	Yes/No

OK—now let's take a look at each of these. While you look at the answers, think about how you could change the learning objective to make it meet both criteria.

Learning Objective	Would do	Can Tell
Learner should be able to identify all the criteria necessary to select the correct product for that client.	Yes, this is probably a real-world task.	Yes, there are a number of relatively simple ways to assess whether the learner can do this.
Learner should be able to list all common Dutch prepositions from memory.	No.	Yes, this would be easy to assess.
Learner should understand project-management roles and responsibilities.	Maybe. The goal is so broad and fuzzy that it's hard to say yes or no definitively.	This would be extremely difficult to assess. It would probably be best to break this learning objective down into smaller objectives.
Learner should be able to create a website that works on the five most common web browsers.	Yes.	Yes.
Learner should be able to state the legal definition of sexual harassment.	No.	Yes, although some clarification would be necessary to say for sure. For example, do you need a word-for-word definition, or just the major criteria?
Learner should be able to identify whether a complaint meets the definition of sexual harassment, and be able to state the reasons why.	Yes, this is a task that someone might need to do in the real world.	Yes.
Learner will understand the limitations of JavaScript as a programming tool.	Not really. It's a little fuzzy and broad, and could be made much clearer.	No.

So if we wanted to fix that last objective, how could we make it better?

Original objective:

Learner will understand the limitations of JavaScript as a programming tool.

A possible revision:

Learner will be able to identify the best programming tools for a specific task and be able to state the reasons why.

Or perhaps:

Learner will be able to state whether or not JavaScript is an appropriate programming tool for a specific task and give a correct rationale for the decision.

There may be times when it's not feasible to have real-world tasks. For example, if you are teaching someone nuclear physics, there may be some conceptual material that just doesn't have an analogous real-world task but that is necessary to understand in order to tackle later concepts. Still, even in those instances, there's probably something the learner is supposed to *do* with the information, even if it's just to use it to understand something else. Also, learning objectives related specifically to motivation gaps may include what learners know or believe.

These recommendations are guidelines, not unimpeachable rules. Use your judgment. If you feel like you need to do backflips to get a learning objective to work, then that's usually a clue that you need to unpack it more—either break it down or keep asking *why* until you've uncovered the real purpose.

HOW SOPHISTICATED SHOULD YOUR LEARNER BE?

When setting your goals, consider how much you want your learner to actually learn. There are a couple of ways to think about this.

The first way is to think about how sophisticated or complex you want your learner's understanding to be. One scale for this is Bloom's Taxonomy (this is the later version, revised by Anderson & Krathwohl in 2001):

- Remember
- Understand
- Apply
- Analyze
- Evaluate
- Create

So, for example, if someone is reading *The Non-Designer's Design Book*, an excellent book on the basics of graphic design, they would learn about the graphic design principles of Contrast, Repetition, Alignment, and Proximity (which adds up to a nicely memorable acronym).

If we looked at this from the perspective of the taxonomy, it might be like this:

Taxonomy	A Way the Learner Might Do This
Remember	Tell somebody what the acronym is and what each item stands for.
Understand	Explain what each principle means.
Apply	Organize the elements of a webpage using the four principles.
Analyze	Look at a print advertisement and explain how each of the four principles is being used in the design.
Evaluate	Expertly critique several different advertisements based on their use of the four principles.
Create	Create a print or web layout from scratch.

The items are intended to become more cognitively demanding as you go (e.g., "remember" should be easier than "evaluate"), and some learning designers view the list as a progression (e.g., you have to understand before you can analyze).

Logically, the idea that this is a progression makes sense, but it's not a recipe for a learning design. For example, analyzing a series of advertisements could be a good way to understand the principles, or guiding learners through the creation of a print advertisement could be a good way to learn an application.

In fact, you could create a great lesson by inverting the order completely:

Taxonomy	A Way the Learner Might Do This
Create	Give the learners some elements (product photo, copy, logo) and have them create a mockup of an advertisement.
Evaluate	Have learners compare their advertisements to a few professional examples, and have them discuss what they did right and wrong.
Analyze	As students are pointing out design elements that work, group those elements on a whiteboard into the four design principles.
Apply	Have the students go back and fix elements in their original advertisement based on the design principles.
Understand	Summarize the design principles, fleshing out the definitions where needed, and correct any misconceptions or address any questions.
Remember	Have the students create their own "cheat sheet" of the four design principles that they can use as a future reference.

TIP: Even if you mix and match the levels as needed, it's still useful to pinpoint the level(s) you're aiming for. For example, if you are teaching someone how to read electrical schematics, you may never need to get beyond Analyze, and if your goal is for learners to apply a concept, you need to make sure your learning design doesn't stop at Understand.

HOW PROFICIENT SHOULD YOUR LEARNER BE?

Another way to look at how much you think your learner should learn is to ask how *proficient* you want your learner to become. There are a number of scales that address this, but I like this one from Gloria Gery (1991):

- Familiarization
- Comprehension
- Conscious Effort
- Conscious Action
- Proficiency
- Unconscious Competence

If we apply this scale to our CRAP example, it might look something like this:

Scale	A Way the Learner Might Show This
Familiarization	Be able to recognize or recall the design principles.
Comprehension	Be able to explain or describe the principles, or recognize examples, if prompted.
Conscious Effort	Attempt to design something by consciously using the principles.
Conscious Action	Successfully design something by consciously using the principles.
Proficiency	Successfully design things using the principles without laborious referencing.
Unconscious Competence	Design using the principles without even thinking about it or deliberately referencing the principles.

By the time you hit unconscious competence with something like the graphic design principles, you are doing things like seeing movie posters out of the corner of your eye and wincing at the misalignment of the text elements. You've fully automated the ideas, and no longer have to put a lot of conscious effort toward the tasks.

Generally it takes quite a bit of time and practice to develop unconscious competence. If you think back to learning how to drive, it probably was months and years before you no longer had to expend a lot of conscious effort on the task. Some of the unconscious driving competencies you might now have probably took years to develop.

It's more unusual to invert this scale, but it can happen. Language learning is an example. You probably have unconscious competence in a number of grammar rules (you do them right without thinking about it) that you couldn't consciously explain.

Another way to think of it is as an XY axis—how sophisticated or complex do you want their understanding to be, and what level of proficiency do you want to get them to?

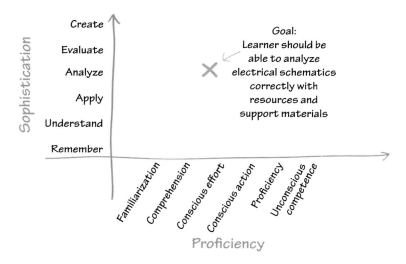

Not surprisingly, the higher you go on either scale, the more time, practice, and skills development you'll need to do. You absolutely cannot get past Conscious Action without a significant amount of practice distributed over time. You also can't get to the higher levels of sophistication without multiple examples, and without the opportunity to interact with those examples and get feedback.

A single exposure to the material will likely only familiarize the learner, or take them just a little bit further than that. If you are being asked to get learners to those higher levels, but being given only one point of contact with the learners (one class session or one elearning course), it almost certainly can't be done.

COMMUNICATING LEARNING OBJECTIVES

One of the "rules" of training is that you tell the learners what the objectives are. When I first started taking instructional design classes, this was handed down as instructional design gospel ("Thou shalt inform learners of the learning objectives!").

That frequently manifests itself as a slide like this at the beginning of training presentations:

Ever seen one of those slides at the beginning of a training class? If not, maybe you blocked it out (I've certainly done that a time or two). If so, I can only hope the learning objectives were a bit better written than these, but why do we announce the learning objectives to our learners in the first place?

There are a few different reasons you might want to tell your learners what the objectives or goals are:

- To focus the learner's attention on the key points in the objectives
- To let learners know what to expect
- To let them know what level of performance they should be working toward

There are other reasons why you, as the learning designer, want to have clear learning objectives as well: You want a clear design direction so you know what you are trying to do (and just as importantly, what you are *not* trying to do), and you want to show a target or benchmark for assessing whether you've succeeded at the end of the project. But again, these learning objectives are more for you as the designer than they are for the learner.

Will Thalheimer, an instructional design expert, has a taxonomy of different types of learning objectives (Thalheimer 2006):

Type	Purpose
Focusing Objective	A statement presented to learners before they encounter learning material, provided to help guide learner attention to the most important aspects of that learning material.
Performance Objective	A statement presented to learners before they encounter learning material, provided to help learners get a quick understanding of the competencies they will be expected to learn.
Instructional-Design Objective	A statement developed by and for instructional designers to guide the design and development of learning and instruction.
Instructional-Evaluation Objective	A statement developed by and for program evaluators (or instructional designers) to guide the evaluation of instruction.

New instructional designers frequently struggle with writing good learning objectives, partly because they are often being asked to cram all four of these functions into a single statement. That's like trying to pack all the gear for a family of four into a single carry-on bag—it's somewhere between difficult and impossible. It also means that learners are subjected to horrible instructional design jargon. That jargon can serve a purpose for the design team in making sure the learning objectives are precise, but it's just cruel to bludgeon your learners with it.

So how might you think about each of these categories?

Type	Ask Yourself	Example
Focusing Objective	Is there something I particularly want to focus the learner's attention on?	"JavaScript can be a useful tool, but it's not right for everything. In this module, you'll want to pay particular attention to how you'll decide whether JavaScript is right for your project."
Performance Objective	What level of proficiency are you going to require from the user, and does the user need to know that's coming?	"Your mission, should you choose to accept it, is to make recommendations back to the team about the five upcoming software projects, and whether JavaScript is the right tool to use. You will need to defend your decision to the team."
Instructional-Design Objective	What goal are you basing your design on?	"Learner will be able to state whether or not JavaScript is an appropriate programming tool for a specific task and give a correct rationale for their decision."
Instructional-Evaluation Objective	A statement developed by and for program evaluators (or instructional designers) to guide the evaluation of instruction	"In scenarios judging the appropriateness of JavaScript, learners will have at least 80% decision-making accuracy, and be able to list from recall at least 75% of the criteria to justify their decisions."

And, for the record, just say no to learning-objective slides at the beginning of the course. If you want to communicate the objectives to the learner, use a challenge, a scenario, or a "your mission, should you choose to accept it" message. There are a multitude of ways that *aren't* bullet points on a slide to accomplish the goals of focusing the learner's attention and letting them know where they are headed.

DETERMINE THE GAP

Once you've set your learning objectives, you want to revisit the question of why learners aren't currently meeting those objectives. What are the gaps between their current situations and where you want them to be?

- Knowledge gaps
- Skills gaps
- Motivation or attitude gaps
- Habit gaps
- Environment gaps
- Communication gaps

So which comes first, the learning objective or the gap? The answer is both, pretty much. It's likely you are starting with some kind of need or challenge, and you are going to want to investigate both learning objectives and performance gaps. There are times when one will inform the other. For example, if you want to train people how to use the super-cool analysis feature in your software, you might have a learning objective about learners being able to run analysis reports. Subsequent gap analysis might tell you that learners do know the procedure for running the reports—they just don't know they can access their own data in the analysis. That would lead you to a very different learning objective.

HOW LONG IS THE TRIP?

When considering a learner's journey, think about how far your learner can really progress along the path.

Years ago I had a fairly blechy job teaching GMAT prep classes. The class met for an entire weekend to prepare prospective MBA students to take the GMAT exam the following weekend.

With a typical student, we stood a decent chance of improving their Quantitative (math, logic, problem-solving) scores, but we usually couldn't make much of a dent in their Verbal scores.

In the Quantitative section, we could teach them some quickie shortcuts for math problems, remind them of the geometry formulas they hadn't seen since their sophomore year of high school, and get them used to the wacky "data sufficiency" format that shows up on the test.

These skills were information-based, based on activation of prior (albeit rusty) knowledge, or very quick to learn, and could therefore be brought to a reasonable level of mastery in a few hours (whether they retained those skills is another matter).

In the Verbal section, they needed skills like vocabulary, reading comprehension, complex analysis, and reasoning. As you might imagine, these are not skills you acquire in a weekend (try decades). There are very few quickie shortcuts that you can teach someone if the foundations of their language skills aren't there.

Some knowledge or skills can be acquired quickly, but others are slow and take a long time to develop.

So how far down the path can a learner go?

I've had clients who told me they want to teach problem-solving skills in a half-hour elearning course.

Since problem-solving is a skill that takes a looooong time to develop, I usually sigh quietly to myself and then tell them a variant of the above story.

Developing Problem-Solving Skills

What can be accomplished in a single e-learning course

WHAT'S PACE LAYERING?

Stewart Brand is the author of a book called *How Buildings Learn: What Happens After They're Built*. In the book, he describes an idea called pace layering.

Basically, the idea is that some things change quickly (the actual contents of the room might change daily, the interior decorating might change in months to years), some things change more slowly (the space usage, the interior layout, and the actual structure might change in years), and some things change only very slowly (the foundation might change in years, decades, or centuries). (Brand 1994)

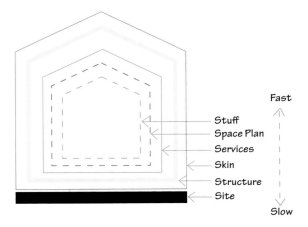

Here's what Mr. Brand says (on the Long Now Foundation site) about the pace layering of cities and civilization:

> *The fast parts learn, propose, and absorb shocks; the slow parts remember, integrate, and constrain. The fast parts get all the attention. The slow parts have all the power.*

This raises the question, What is the pace layering of learners? What can change quickly, and what changes more slowly?

In the GMAT course I taught, we could—at best—rearrange some furniture (and hope that it stayed rearranged until they took the test the following week). We weren't going to really change anything like their verbal skills—those were part of the structure and foundation.

FAST OR SLOW?

If a particular learning point is fast, you might be able to get your learner all the way from beginning to end. If it's something very slow, like their problem-solving skills, you'll be lucky to inch them down the path.

Take a look at this example. Todd is a brand-new restaurant manager. He just got promoted, and he needs to get his skills up to par as quickly as possible. Which of the skills that Todd needs to acquire are fast? Which are slow?

Todd, a brand-new manager

Todd's New Job Requirements

Competencies	Fast or Slow?
Approve timesheets	Fast - - - - - - - - - - Slow
Communicate changes & updates to staff	Fast - - - - - - - - - - Slow
Create weekly schedules	Fast - - - - - - - - - - Slow
Design & implement creative seasonal promotions	Fast - - - - - - - - - - Slow
Ensure a respectful environment	Fast - - - - - - - - - - Slow
Forecast inventory requirements	Fast - - - - - - - - - - Slow
Minimize waste	Fast - - - - - - - - - - Slow
Perform monthly check of security & sprinkler systems	Fast - - - - - - - - - - Slow
Recognize & prevent harassment in the workplace	Fast - - - - - - - - - - Slow
Recognize & reward employees	Fast - - - - - - - - - - Slow
Resolve employee conflicts	Fast - - - - - - - - - - Slow
Train on proper procedures for safe alcohol sales	Fast - - - - - - - - - - Slow
Verify that tables are set properly	Fast - - - - - - - - - - Slow

Loosely speaking, approving timesheets, communicating changes, checking security and sprinkler systems, and verifying table settings are probably pretty fast skills. Creating weekly schedules, designing and implementing creative seasonal promotions, recognizing and preventing harassment, and training on safe alcohol sales are probably medium or mixed sets of skills, and things like ensuring a respectful environment, forecasting inventory requirements, minimizing waste, recognizing and rewarding employees, and resolving employee conflicts are slow skills.

Fast skills typically have more explicit rule sets. Faster skills tend to be things where you can make a list of the right answers. Slower skills tend to be things that have more tacit rule sets—it's hard to say what "right" is, but you might know it when you see it. So, for example, table setting is pretty explicit—you could explain what the rules are—but ensuring a respectful environment is harder to define as explicitly. When a skill is based on tacit rules, it's usually necessary for the learner to see lots of examples so that she or he can start to recognize patterns.

So what can you do with this? If you identify that something is a slow task, how do you approach it?

Find a few throw pillows. What are some easy, cheap ways to make an impact? It might be a model, a tool, a job aid, a checklist—something that's easy for your learners to implement right away and that will have an immediate impact. It won't change their world, but it might solve a small but pesky problem. Don't try to solve big problems with a throw pillow, though. They may brighten the room and be a cheap way to have an impact (and there's nothing wrong with that), but they aren't a substitute for the heavy lifting involved in real behavioral change.

Provide some sturdier pieces. Give them some more concrete material, but recognize that this is going to take more time; they will need to set it up, move it into place, get rid of the old piece, arrange their existing stuff in it, and get used to how it changes their current patterns. Don't try to do that all at once; keep in mind that there are several steps and that all of them need to be supported, unless you want the unassembled item sitting in its box in the storage area indefinitely.

Recognize that you aren't going to change their structure. If they have some renovations already in place, you might move them along a little, or you can help them start some planning for future changes. This sounds easy, but actually it's really hard, because it involves letting go of the deeply held belief that we can do major renovations in a short period of time. We can't—and it's a waste of resources to pretend we can. If we approach a learning design with the longer view in mind, acknowledging what we can and cannot accomplish, we can create better ways to help people and ensure that there is a long-term plan.

Respect the foundation. The foundation is based on a learner's personal bedrock, which is composed of elements like culture and personality. If your structural changes aren't going to sit well on the foundation, then you are better off changing your design, because it's really unlikely that the foundation is going anywhere.

DESIGNING FOR FAST AND SLOW

So how do you design for this? If something is fast, then that's pretty easy. You present the concept, make sure the learner has adequate opportunity to practice it, and reinforce it as necessary. Slow skills are really the problem. What do you do if it's a slow skill?

Let's take a look at the management skill of hiring the right people. That can be a pretty slow skill to develop. People who have been managers for 20 years can still be learning new things and getting better at this.

What can we do to help Todd improve his skills in this area?

Speed	Type	What You Can Do
Very Fast	Tools, checklists, specific procedures	Give Todd a checklist of hiring questions, and practice using and evaluating the answers. Have Todd use the list as a job aid while he's interviewing.
Moderate	Skills, practice, proficiency development	Practice scenarios and role-plays of hiring situations, spaced out over time with detailed feedback.
Slow	Higher-level conceptual and strategic skills, expert coaching, extensive practice	Have Todd receive expert coaching from an experienced manager. Also have him read and study deeper resources in the area and set personal development goals in this area.
Foundation	Evaluation, self-assessment, awareness	Have Todd assess his own skills, personality, and cultural biases, and how these things impact his abilities as a manager. Todd is unlikely to change those things, but learning to be aware of them can help him accept and work with them beneficially.

SUMMARY

- Use questions like "Why, why, no really, why?" and "What bad thing will happen if they don't know?" to uncover the real reason for learning.
- Define the problem before coming up with solutions, to ensure you are actually solving the real problem and not a problem you *don't* have.
- Use the two questions "Is this something the learner would actually do in the real world?" and "Can I tell when they've done it?" to make sure your learning objectives are useful and usable.
- Decide how sophisticated your learners' understanding needs to be and how proficient they need to be, and then design accordingly.
- Recognize if you are teaching someone a fast or slow skill, and use strategies appropriate to developing that type of skill.

REFERENCES

Anderson, Lorin W. and David Krathwohl, eds. 2001. *A Taxonomy for Learning, Teaching, and Assessing: A Revision of Bloom's Taxonomy of Educational Objectives, complete edition.* New York: Longman.

Bloom, Benjamin S. 1956. *Taxonomy of Educational Objectives, Handbook I: The Cognitive Domain.* New York: David McKay Co Inc.

Brand, Stewart. 1994. *How Buildings Learn: What Happens After They're Built.* New York: Viking.

Gery, Gloria. 1991. *Electronic Performance Support Systems: How and Why to Remake the Workplace Through the Strategic Application of Technology.* Boston: Weingarten Publications.

Thalheimer, Will. 2006. "New Taxonomy for Learning Objectives," *Will At Work Learning Blog,* June 1. www.willatworklearning.com/2006/06/new_taxonomy_fo.html.

HOW DO WE REMEMBER?

(IN WHICH WE LEARN THAT MEMORY IS MESSY
AND THAT BIKING STRAIGHT UPHILL
ISN'T A GOOD WAY TO LEARN)

Memory is the foundation of learning, so let's take a few pages to talk about how learners actually learn and remember stuff. How does all that knowledge get in there on any given day? And how do we find and retrieve it when we need it?

There's a lot we still don't know about the nature of memory, but we do have some ideas and models for how it works. First, we'll look at how we pay attention and encode information into memory. Second, we'll look at different types of memory.

MEMORY IN & OUT

Successful learning involves encoding and retrieval—memory in and memory out. Remembering is a necessary first step, but you need to be able to retrieve, manipulate, combine, and innovate with the information you remember.

Information in your brain doesn't just sit there like a wool sweater during summertime. When you put information in, it doesn't lie passively waiting to be taken out but instead interacts with other information. So your brain isn't *really* a closet.

In order for your brain to be like a closet, it would have to be a super-automated closet that reorganizes itself constantly, or one that's populated by some kind of closet elves who are continually moving and arranging things.

Also, anything you put in your closet automatically gets stored in multiple categories, so the blue socks your grandmother knitted for you would simultaneously (and magically) be put with things that are wool, things that are blue, socks, outfits that go with those socks, stuff from Grandma, things that are starting to wear out, and so on.

What's more, the self-organizing closet has multiple, overlapping ways to keep track of things. So when you put away those blue socks in the "socks" drawer, the closet can retrieve them by looking on the "things that are wool" shelf or on the "things that are blue" hanger.

Your brain is a dynamic, multi-faceted, constantly changing entity. Anything you retain from this book will change the physical structure of your brain by creating new connections and strengthening (or weakening) existing connections.

So what winds up sticking? We are bombarded with millions and millions of data points all day long. We can't possibly attend to—much less remember—all of them.

Fortunately, you have a series of filters and triggers that allows you to parse this information:

- **Sensory memory.** This type of memory is your first filter of everything you sense and perceive. If you choose to pay attention to something, it gets passed on to short-term memory.
- **Short-term memory.** This is the memory that allows you to hold on to ideas or thoughts long enough to take action. Most things get discarded out of short-term memory, but some things get encoded into long-term memory.
- **Long-term memory.** This is your closet, where you store information that you'll keep for a while.

Let's take a closer look at each of these.

SENSORY MEMORY

The first level of memory is sensory memory. Basically pretty much anything you sense is held momentarily in your sensory memory.

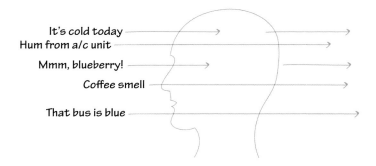

Most sensations keep right on going, unless there's something unusual or note-worthy about what you are sensing.

For example, stop right now and pay attention to all the noises you can hear. If you are indoors, you are likely hearing the hum of an air conditioning or heating unit, or noise from appliances or computers. If you are outside, there will be environmental noises depending on your location.

Unless someone or something calls your attention to one of these, you probably weren't paying attention to those noises, and you were certainly not encoding those noises into your memory.

HABITUATION

Sensory memory isn't a big concern for learning designers, except for the phenomenon of habituation. Habituation means getting used to a sensory stimulus to the point that we no longer notice or respond to it.

> **HABITUATION:** This allows you to stop noticing the annoying refrigerator buzz after you've been listening to it for a while, or when you stop even noticing that "check engine" light on the dashboard when it's been on for weeks.

If things are unpredictable, they can be harder to habituate to. For example, the horrible torment of a flickering fluorescent light persists long after you've stopped hearing the hum from the computer monitor, because the unpredictable pattern of the flicker keeps calling our attention to it over and over and over…

Similarly, being stuck in traffic stays infuriating because it's rarely uniform (start…stop…start…little faster…STOP…go…go go…Go…GOGOGOGO… *Stooooop*!).

People can also habituate to things that we don't necessarily want them to habituate to. For example, when was the last time you paid much attention to the advertisements in the banner at the top of webpages? You've probably learned how to tune those out. Web designers refer to that as "banner blindness," and eye-tracking studies (Nielsen 2007) verify that not only do people not pay much attention to banner ads, but they frequently don't look at them at all. (The same thing can happen with resource and reference material we provide for learners on websites and in elearning courses!)

IMPLICATIONS FOR LEARNING DESIGN

Consistency can be useful. Consistency can be a useful tool to make things easier for your learner. For example, if you use the same basic format for each chapter of a technical manual, your learners get used to the format and don't have to expend mental energy repeatedly orienting themselves to the format; instead, they can focus on the *content* of the chapters.

Too much consistency is bad. Too much consistency can lead to habituation in your learners. You want to vary your teaching methods and the way you present information. For example, if you are creating an elearning program and you give the same type of feedback in the same location every single time, then learners are going to learn to ignore it, particularly if the feedback is the generic "Good Job!" kind. Another example of too much consistency is the "banner blindness" mentioned above.

Annoying variability is bad too. While some variation is useful for keeping the learner's attention, meaningless differences are just irritating. For example, if you take that elearning feedback box and have it randomly pop up in different areas of the screen, it will probably keep the learner from habituating to it as quickly, but it's also going to really annoy them. A better approach would be to have different feedback formats that are appropriate to the different types of content you are presenting, or to use a variety of different learning activities to keep things interesting. Variation can be a useful tool for maintaining attention, but it should be used in a deliberate and meaningful way.

The best way to know whether something is too consistent is through user testing. Watch your learners interact with print or electronic materials, or pilot test a class—if your learners are inattentive or seem to obviously ignore resource materials, that's a clue that they've started to gloss past those elements.

SHORT-TERM OR WORKING MEMORY

Once something has attracted your attention, it moves into your short-term or working memory. If it succeeds in penetrating your short-term memory, it's probably something that:

- Is significant to you for some reason
- You are actively looking for
- You need to take action on
- Surprises or confounds your expectations

Working memory has a relatively short duration and limited capacity, but you use it pretty much constantly throughout the day.

WHAT DO YOU RETAIN?

For example, let's say you are deciding what to wear to work today. You glance at the weather (cool and rainy) and at your schedule (client meeting). You hold those two things in working memory while you check your closet. You also retrieve some information from long-term memory (the conference room is always hot; the black suit is at the cleaners because of that unfortunate guacamole stain).

New Information in Working Memory	Pulled from Long-Term Memory
Cool and rainy weather	Conference room is always hot
Client meeting	Black suit is at the cleaners

All this information gets processed together as you make the decision to wear layers.

Working memory will discard most pieces of information as soon as you're done with them, like the Wi-Fi password at the coffee shop, the number of the freeway exit you need to take, or the phone number that you recite over and over until you can get it dialed.

All of those types of information are the kind of thing that you might keep in working memory for the few seconds that you will need it. If it takes you longer, you might also keep it there via repetition.

"I need to take exit 42a" → [action] → forget

Repetition will refresh the information in working memory until you use it and stop repeating. If you repeat something long enough, you will eventually grind it into long-term memory, but that's not the most efficient method (we'll discuss better methods later). Some information will drop out more quickly if it doesn't have significance.

Let's take a look at the following three pieces of information you might hear in the morning news radio report.

Information: The temperature is 12 degrees Celsius.

Factors that influence retention:

- Is it unusual? If it's significantly different than the weather for the last few days, it's more likely to catch your attention.
- Is it important to you? You'll retain it better if the weather affects your plans for the day.
- Is it a familiar format? If you ordinarily use Fahrenheit, you're unlikely to remember the Celsius temperature, because you won't know whether it means you should wear your coat.

If you do remember it for the length of the day, it's still unlikely you'll continue to remember it days or weeks later, unless there was something significant about the date (e.g., it was your brother's wedding day).

Information: The Dow Jones industrial average is up 56 points, or 0.5 percent, to 11,781.

Factors that influence retention: The same issues apply. Does this contrast with previous days or expectations? Is this significant to you because you work with the financial markets or are waiting to sell some stock?

Information: UConn Huskies lost to the Stanford Cardinal 71–59.

Factors that influence retention: You are likely to retain this information only if you follow US women's college basketball, or if you know that this was the first game the UConn team had lost after setting the record for the most consecutive games won (89). If you don't have that context, or if that score isn't meaningful to you in some other way, you probably won't retain any part of that information.

WHAT'S THE LIMIT?

How much can you hold in working memory? There is a fair amount of research on the limits of working memory, and there's a well-known statistic about 7±2 items in working memory, but the real answer is *it depends*. (Miller 1956)

In all likelihood, you can't repeat all the data from the previous table (the temperature, the Dow Jones numbers, and the sports scores) without going back and checking it again. The main reason you can't is because those numbers have no significance for you, beyond being examples in this book.

An additional reason would be the quantity of information—there were several discrete facts in that table (12°, Celsius, Dow Jones, 56 points, 0.5%, 11, 781, UConn Huskies, Stanford Cardinal, 71, 59). That's more pieces of individual information than most people can remember without some kind of memory aid or device.

Read this number, and then close your eyes and try to repeat it:

6 7 1 8

How'd you do? In all likelihood you did pretty well at retaining that briefly. Four discrete digits is usually well within the limits of working memory.

Now try this number:

  9 3 4 8 7 1 6 2 5

That one is a little harder, right? Maybe you were
able to retain all nine digits, but if you dropped some
digits they were likely to be somewhere in the middle
of the string of numbers. That would be an example
of primacy and recency effects, which suggest we are
more likely to remember something at the beginning
of a sequence or list (primacy) and also more likely to
remember the most recent things, as at the end of a
list (recency).

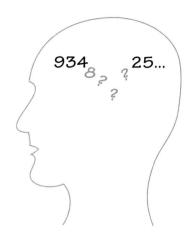

OK, now try this one:

  100 500 800

That's a whole lot easier, right? It's the same number of digits, but it's *chunked*.
Instead of remembering individual digits, you are remembering something
like this:

  [first three digits] + [next three digits] + [last three digits]

This is three chunks of information, rather than nine separate chunks of
information.

Even easier is:

  1 2 3 4 5 6 7 8 9

Because you already know how to count to nine, this is just one chunk of
information for you:

  [digits 1–9 in order]

Chunking can be based on things that are similar, sequential, or items that are
in your long-term memory.

For example, try this number:

  612 651 763 952

In all likelihood, this is too much information for you to retain in working memory,
unless you live in the Minneapolis/St. Paul area, where these are the local telephone area codes.

WHAT DOES THIS MEAN FOR LEARNING DESIGN?

Who memorizes strings of numbers anymore? Doesn't everybody have a cellphone?

We are fortunate to have devices we can use to offload tedious details, and most people don't have any need to remember random strings of numbers (which is a good thing, because humans mostly suck at that particular task, whereas electronic devices are brilliant at it).

But using chunking in learning—whether it involves large numbers or large amounts of textual or perhaps even visual information—will help your learners manage their working memory, and help them understand where to focus their limited attention at any given point.

Let's say you are teaching somebody a procedure—for example, how to bake an apple pie. Take a look at this list of steps:

Mix together the flour and the salt.

Chill the butter and water.

Add the butter to the flour and cut it with a pastry blender until it resembles coarse crumbs.

Add enough water until the dough barely hangs together.

Cut the dough in half and make two balls.

Wrap the dough in plastic wrap and refrigerate.

Peel the apples.

Core and quarter the apples and cut into 1/4-inch slices.

Mix the apples with sugar, lemon juice, cinnamon, and a small amount of flour.

Roll out one of the pieces of pie dough into a circle slightly larger than your pie pan.

Fold the pie dough in half and lift it into the pie pan.

Press the dough into the pan.

Fill the pie dough with the apple mixture.

Roll the other piece of dough into a circle.

Place the dough on top of the pie and crimp the edges.

Cut steam holes in the top crust.

Bake the pie for 45 minutes in a 350° oven.

That's a lot of steps, right? A bit much for someone to process. If they know a lot about baking, they'll be able to parse that information in a way that makes sense, but if the learner doesn't have a lot of context for pie-making, then this list is likely to overwhelm them quickly.

There's no cue to tell them when to stop reading the new information for a moment and process the existing information. There's also no higher-level organization for the material—it's just a long list of steps. Which is why you want to look for opportunities to chunk that information:

Prepare the dough

Mix together the flour and the salt.

Chill the butter and water.

Add the butter to the flour and cut it with a pastry blender until it resembles coarse crumbs.

Add enough water until the dough barely hangs together.

Cut the dough in half and make two balls.

Wrap the dough in plastic wrap and refrigerate.

Prepare the filling

Peel the apples.

Core and quarter the apples and cut into 1/4-inch slices.

Mix the apples with sugar, lemon juice, cinnamon, and a small amount of flour.

Assemble the pie

Roll out one of the pieces of pie dough into a circle slightly larger than your pie pan.

Fold the pie dough in half and lift it into the pie pan.

Press the dough into the pan.

Fill the pie dough with the apple mixture.

Roll the other piece of dough into a circle.

Place the dough on top of the pie and crimp the edges.

Bake the pie

Cut steam holes in the top crust.

Bake the pie for 45 minutes in a 350° oven.

Even just chunking the steps into four categories makes the whole procedure much easier for people to process and remember. Chunking isn't magically going to allow the learner to remember the whole recipe, but it will help them to focus on a single section at any one time, and the steps in an individual chunk are a more realistic quantity of information to hold in working memory.

Working memory acts as a gatekeeper for long-term memory, so if the initial information overloads working memory, it's unlikely to make the transition to long-term memory.

LONG-TERM MEMORY, OR IS IT IN YOUR CLOSET?

Ultimately, when we are teaching or learning something, what we really want is for the information to reach long-term memory—firmly situated in the closet, in a place where we can find it again easily.

WHERE DO YOU PUT IT?

Anything that you do remember becomes part of a series of associations—you don't learn anything in isolation.

For example, say you've just learned that the German word for *mustache* is *Schnurrbart*. Now, in all likelihood, you don't care about this information, and you will let it wash out of your short-term memory without a ripple.

But suppose there is some reason you need to retain this information (a German vocabulary test, a fascination with words that sound like sneezes, an interest in European facial hair trends). How will you encode it? Well, of course, that depends on the shape of your closet and the types of shelves that you have for that information. Fortunately, you don't have to choose a single association— you can store this item on all of those shelves simultaneously.

More (and better) associations will make it easier to retrieve the information. If you don't have a good shelving system for this word, you can create a mnemonic for it (tell yourself a story about sitting across from a German man with an elaborate mustache while riding the Bay Area Rapid Transit (BART) system, for example).

If you already speak German, you probably wouldn't need a mnemonic, as you'd already have a much more sophisticated shelving system for this word, involving the root meanings of the parts of the word ("bart" means beard in German), or other associations.

Your ability to retrieve information depends on the condition and contents of the shelves it's stored on in your mental closet.

MULTIPLE SHELVES

The more ways you have to find a piece of information, the easier it is to retrieve, so an item that goes on only one or two shelves is going to be harder to retrieve than an item that goes on many shelves.

For example, let's take two five-digit numbers: My mother's zip code and the salary offer I had for my first job after graduate school.

I don't have many shelves for the first number:

MY MOTHER'S ZIPCODE
Zipcodes I know

I don't use this number very often, and I don't have very many ways to access the information (I either remember it or I don't). In fact, these days I don't actually remember it, and have to get it from one of the external resources I use to supplement my memory (like an address book or a contact file on my phone). Basically, I have only one place to look for that number, and if that doesn't work, I don't have any other way to retrieve that information.

The salary offer, however, was a number with a lot more significance (sorry, Mom) and could be put on quite a few more shelves.

SALARY OFFER
What I'd like to earn

SALARY OFFER
What I thought other people earned

SALARY OFFER
What I earn now

SALARY OFFER
What I was earning before

As a result, I have multiple ways to access that information. I know it was almost twice what I was making before I went to graduate school, it was 10 percent less than a friend of mine made with the same degree (she was a much better negotiator), and I know how it compares to my current salary.

The more shelves you can put an item on, the more likely that you'll be able to retrieve it in the future. This is the problem with pure memorization tasks such as flash cards—things you've learned that way tend to be on only one shelf (the "things you've memorized" shelf), which makes them harder to retrieve.

POORLY CONSTRUCTED SHELVES

Some of my shelves are pretty weak, and they allow information to slip through. For example, I was trying to learn some Japanese before a trip a few years ago. Instead of a sturdy wooden shelf, my shelf for Japanese vocabulary was more like a rickety wire rack—I would carefully balance a few words and phrases there, but they'd frequently slip through, and I wouldn't find them when I went back to retrieve something.

Part of the reason my shelf for Japanese was so rickety was because I had so little context for Japanese. If I were trying to learn Spanish, I would have a sturdier shelf for that language despite being a novice at it. My Spanish shelf would be strengthened by all the context I have for Spanish (things like similar Latin roots to some words in English, a close relationship to Italian, which I do know a little, and years of watching Spanish language vocabulary cartoons on *Sesame Street* as a child).

CROWDED SHELVES

A shelf that is crowded may not be specific enough. That can happen when you have a lot of information but not a very sophisticated structure for organizing that information. It makes it much more difficult to retrieve items accurately.

For example, my shelf for jazz music is pretty crowded, not because I know a lot about jazz (I don't), but rather because everything I do know about jazz— a specific artist name, that one piece that always makes me smile, the time period in which a certain style of jazz was born—pretty much gets crammed on a single shelf labeled "Jazz." This means I have a really hard time retrieving specific information about jazz.

My shelves for '80s popular music, on the other hand, are embarrassingly well developed. There are shelves for different genres, for American groups, British groups, hair bands, Americana, MTV, music videos, stuff I owned on LP, stuff I owned on cassette, bands I saw in concert, and so on (too bad you can't just deliberately choose to "unlearn" things).

UNINTENDED SHELVES

Sometimes associations are unintended. For example, a few years ago I was in Washington, DC, staying a few blocks away from the Fannie Mae building while the mortgage association was being heavily discussed in the news. There was a lush bed of lavender plants in front of the building, and you couldn't walk by without smelling lavender.

Now, the Federal National Mortgage Association is forever on my lavender shelf (and vice versa).

This happens far more often than we realize. Our brain creates numerous associations that we may or may not be aware of, utilizing all our senses (sight, sound, touch, taste, and smell).

While these associations are somewhat random, they are still part of the associations we use to retrieve information. Let's take a look at how those associations can actually be used.

IN-CONTEXT LEARNING

Pop quiz: You are taking a class at the local university and have an in-class exam the next week. Where is the best place to study for a test?

a. Outside under a tree in peaceful sunshine
b. In your gray, windowless classroom with a noisy air conditioning system
c. In a quiet, well-lit library
d. In a noisy coffee shop

The answer may be surprising: it's B, the gray, windowless classroom. Yes, the one with the noisy air conditioning system. Why? Because the environment in which you study will become part of your association with the material you are studying. When possible, you want to encode the information in the same type of environment where you will also be retrieving that information.

The same is true for information that needs to be retrieved in a particular context, such as on the job. The farther the learning is from the context of use, the fewer shelves are being utilized to store the information.

The context of the classroom is only helping you remember if you need to retrieve that information in a classroom. But we learn all sorts of information in classrooms that we need to apply later. Topics like plumbing and journalism and geology and hazardous materials handling are all taught in environments that are very different from the environments where those subjects will be used.

We have a tendency to hold classes in bare rooms far away from the place that use is going to happen, and that is a disservice to learners.

Deep down, we know this is true. Whenever lives are at stake, training almost always involves in-context learning. Even if the context is simulated—for the safety of the students or those around them—it's a rich, realistic context. Examples of in-context learning include flight simulators, teaching hospitals, and actual driving practice during driver's education.

If possible, you want to encode the information in the same type of environment where you will also be retrieving that information.

Isn't it inconceivable that drivers' education wouldn't involve actually road time? We wouldn't ever think someone could be a safe driver until they had actual experience driving in real traffic. Eventually simulators may be good enough and cheap enough to replace road practice, but for now, we take it for granted that learning to drive involves practice in the real context.

So why is out-of-context training acceptable in other circumstances? Frequently, it's a matter of convenience or cost or practicality. These can be very real constraints. For example, it might be nice to teach a server administration class in your actual server room, but you just can't get 30 people into a room the size of a large closet.

When practical constraints require that the learning can't happen in the physical space, there are still ways to increase the context. For example, if the class is about the physical setup of computer servers, it should involve hands-on contact with the equipment, even if it can't take place in the server room.

Many times, though, learning happens in an out-of-context environment like a bare, featureless classroom because of habit, tradition, or lack of awareness.

There are a variety of ways to make learning more in-context, despite practical constraints.

Think about ways you might improve or increase the context for learning experiences in the following scenarios:

SCENARIO 1: DEVICE FEATURES

You need to teach consumers about the features of a new cellphone.

How would you make this a high-context experience? Consider how you might do it before reading the answer below.

—TAKE A MOMENT TO CONSIDER WHAT YOU WOULD DO BEFORE MOVING ON—

Ideally, the learner would be interacting with those features on the actual phone as part of the learning experience, and would be trying them out. Additionally, anything that could be done to make the features part of actual use scenarios tailored to the audience would enhance context. So the learning experience would be real tasks that someone would do (texting a friend, entering a work contact) rather than just a guided tour of the features. ■

SCENARIO 2: EATING WELL

You've been given the task of teaching college students how to make nutritionally balanced meals. What can you do to increase the context for this learning experience?

—TAKE A MOMENT TO CONSIDER WHAT YOU WOULD DO BEFORE MOVING ON—

The learning experience should match the final setting as much as possible, which could mean operating in a cruddy dorm kitchen, using cheap cooking equipment from the local chain store, and reflecting the actual food scenarios. Another option would be to use photos of actual student refrigerators and challenge your learners to identify ways to make a healthy meal from the contents.   ■

SCENARIO 3: COMMUNICATION SKILLS

You are creating a course to teach fast-food restaurant managers how to give employees constructive feedback. How would you make this learning experience high context?

—TAKE A MOMENT TO CONSIDER WHAT YOU WOULD DO BEFORE MOVING ON—

Consider in what setting the feedback would take place, and use role-playing to practice. For example, you could have managers create triggers for themselves by doing a mental tour of the restaurant and thinking about what behaviors they would praise at each station. They could create a checklist for themselves of what to look for, where to look for it, and what to do if they see it.   ■

EMOTIONAL CONTEXT

One of the most difficult types of context to create for learning situations is emotional context.

Let's take the employee feedback example. Let's say you are in a class with other students, and you are learning the principles of giving difficult feedback. What's the mood like in the classroom? Everybody is probably calm, and nobody is upset. People are being serious and thoughtful, as befits a classroom environment.

Now, think about the environment when you have to use what you learned. There's a good chance you are nervous, maybe anxious. The person you are talking to is probably unhappy, upset, or even hostile.

So, I wanted to talk to you about these areas for potential improvement...

Sure, I can see how that could really help...

How It's Supposed to Go

So, I had a few things...mostly you do a great job...but...well, there are a few things we should discuss...

Why is this the first time I'm hearing about this?! Why didn't you bring it up before???

How It Actually Goes

In this instance, the emotional context while learning about the material and then while applying it are very different. Many things seem reasonable when we are learning about them—such as, when dealing with a hostile employee, staying calm, using "I" statements, validating the other person's point of view, and so on.

But then you are actually confronted with a really angry person, and all that good advice flies out of your head, and fight-or-flight reactions surge to the front and you couldn't compose a validating "I" statement if your life depended on it.

We may be prepared with the knowledge and the protocols but unable to implement them in the unfamiliar emotional context.

During Learning

During Application

I believe this is why a lot of learning fails. Have you ever said to yourself "I *knew* the right thing to do, but..." The difference between knowing and doing can be a huge gap when the context of encoding and the context of retrieval are significantly different.

There are many things we learn where the emotional context for use is drastically different than the emotional context for learning. We can be trying to retrieve the information when we are in a stressed or otherwise heightened emotional state:

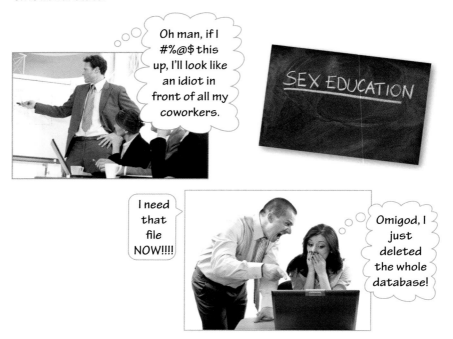

Stressful or emotionally heightened circumstances can cause us to rely less on our intellectual knowledge and more on our automatic responses. This makes it more difficult to transfer something learned in a placid emotional context to a fraught emotional context.

So how can you create proper and effective emotional contexts? There are several ways:

- **Use role-playing.** Even though we know it's not real, role-playing can be an effective way to create the feel of the emotional context, especially if you have someone effective playing the part. Even though it won't be exactly the same, just having practiced saying the words out loud make them easier to recall in real-life situations.
- **Create pressure.** Even if the pressure is different, sometimes adding elements of similar pressure can create similar feelings. For example, a tight time limit on responses can create time pressure, which can approximate the emotional

context of other types of pressure. You need to be careful, however. A little pressure sharpens the learner's attention and alertness, but high amounts of pressure and stress can block new learning. If the environment where the learner needs to perform is very stressful (e.g., emergency situations), it's likely that the learner will need to practice in a lower-stress environment before moving to higher-stress environments.

- **Invest in high-quality stories, acting, and performance.** If it's critical material, get good actors or voice actors and establish a strong emotional setup.

ENCODING FOR RETRIEVAL, OR HOW WILL IT NEED TO BE USED?

One of the things you will also want to consider is how the information will need to be used when it's retrieved. Will the learners only need to recognize the information, will they need to recall it outright, or will they need to be able to use it to actually do something?

That's the option I need.

Recognize?

The options are as follows…

Recall?

If we change out the options offered, we'll increase sales by 5%.

Integrate and Use?

You want the information encoding to align with assessment and use.

If someone is just going to need to recognize the right answer, then recognition activities are good ways to learn and practice. If someone needs to recall something unprompted, then they will need to learn and practice by recalling, not just by recognizing.

Which question is easier to answer?

> **Question 1:** The French word for pool is _____. (fill in the blank)

> **Question 2:** The French word for pool is:
> a) Roman   b) Piscine   c) Plage   d) Plume

The second question is easier, right? *Recognizing* the right answer from a set of options almost always involves less effort than *recalling* the answer.

Learning experiences frequently rely heavily on recognition activities such as multiple-choice questions. This is particularly true in elearning, where the computer is used to evaluate the correctness of student answers. This is primarily a practical choice. Recognition activities are easier to grade—computers can do it for us. Recall activities usually require a person to evaluate.

RECALL: A PRACTICAL EXAMPLE

Look at the examples on the facing page for practicing and assessing a learner's CPR proficiency. Are they good examples? Why or why not? Stop and decide which one is the best before reading further.

CPR requires *recall*—remembering the right steps and how to do them properly. None of the activities you see here are really recall activities. They are mostly recognition activities.

The simulation comes the closest, but you can still simply guess. Also, the context is problematic—it's very different to click on the virtual chest of a patient on a computer screen rather than to apply pressure to an actual patient.

These learning activities might be *part* of a good learning experience, but they don't actually allow the learner to practice recalling the steps in the way that they will need to in a real-life situation.

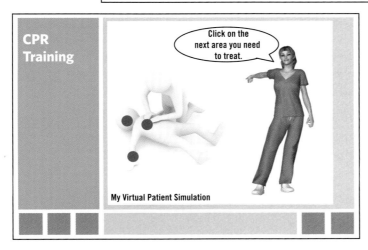

So how can you create learning activities that are a better match for the real-world application?

- Ensure that the practice involves recall or application.

Do you know all the steps?

Test yourself:

Recall Activity

Put the steps in the right order:

Give two breaths   _____

Check pulse   _____

Clear airway   _____

Call 911   _____

Begin compressions   _____

Tilt head   _____

Recognition Activity

- Ensure that the practice and assessment are high-context.

- Use job aids to change something from a recall to a recognition task. Job aids change the task from "recall the steps" to "follow these steps," reducing the need to rely on memory. If you do use job aids, give your learners a chance to practice with the job aid as part of the learning. We'll talk more about this in later chapters.

In the end, the practice needs to match the eventual use. If the learner just needs enough familiarity to recognize the right option, then practicing with recognition activities will be sufficient. If the learner needs to recall the material, or to do something more sophisticated like integrate the material, then the practice activities need to reflect that eventual use.

REAL VS. PERCEIVED KNOWLEDGE

Frequently we think we know something because we recognize it—we *think* we know more than we actually *do* know.

What I think I know

What I actually know

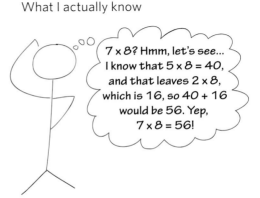

So my conviction that I know the multiplication tables is a little suspect. I apparently know some parts of the multiplication tables, and I know some strategies for extending that knowledge (which is fortunate, because I would apparently be multiplication-illiterate without those strategies).

Let's say you are studying for an exam. You are chewing your pencil, reading your textbook, and nodding—it all looks pretty familiar. You've been studying like that for a while, and you are feeling pretty good about the whole thing.

Then you get to class, and you see this:

Recognition knowledge—the kind that might have gotten you through a multiple-choice test—is suddenly inadequate in the face of a mostly blank sheet of paper.

If you want to eventually retrieve information from your memory, you need to *practice* retrieving it when you study (Karpicke 2011). Retrieval practice has been well studied and is one of the most effective study methods, found in one study to be more effective than traditional studying or mind-mapping.

When you are teaching, you need to make sure that your learning activities allow your learners to practice in the same way that they will need to perform.

TYPES OF MEMORY

So far, we've been talking generally about the way a stimulus gets encoded into long-term memory, but there isn't just one general type of memory. There are actually several different types of memory that are encoded and retrieved in distinct ways. Some types of memory will be more appropriate to focus on, depending on your subject matter, and learning design can often benefit from taking advantage of different types of memory.

There's a well-known story in psychology about an amnesia patient who did not have the ability to form new explicit memories. Her doctor had to reintroduce himself to her every time they met, because she couldn't remember him from day to day.

One day, as an experiment, the doctor hid a small sharp object in his hand when he shook the patient's hand in greeting.

When he followed up with her later, she had no explicit memory of meeting him, and needed to be introduced to him yet again, but when he offered his hand, she didn't want to shake it, even though, when asked, she couldn't give any reason for her reluctance.

This suggests that memories are processed in different ways, and that people are not consciously aware of all their memories.

What you know you know—The overlapping area (above) is your explicit memory. You know it and you know you know it, and you can talk about it if needed.

What you don't know you know—The rest of the blue area is your *tacit* memory. You know it, but you couldn't describe it in any detail or talk about it in a meaningful way. Sometimes it is things you forgot you knew, and other times it is things that are encoded in memory without your conscious awareness. You don't need to be an amnesiac to have tacit knowledge.

What you only *think* you know—The yellow area is made up of things you only think you know, but when you try to use those bits, your knowledge is incomplete or reconstructed incorrectly. Everybody has this—it's part of the messy human cognition process.

Within these categories, there are many different types of memory. We are still very much in the process of understanding how different types of memory work in the brain, but some of the types of memory include:

- **Declarative or semantic memory.** This is stuff you can talk about—facts, principles, or ideas, like WWII ending in 1945 or your zip code.
- **Episodic memory.** This is also a form of declarative memory, but it's specific to stories or recollections from your own experience, like what happened at your graduation or when you started your first job.
- **Conditioned memory.** Like Pavlov's dog, we all have conditioned reactions to certain triggers, whether we realize it or not, like when a pet gets excited about the sound of the can opener that precedes getting fed.
- **Procedural memory.** This is memory for how to perform procedures, like driving a car or playing the piano.
- **Flashbulb memories.** We seem to have a special type of memory for highly emotionally charged events, like national catastrophes.

Each different type of memory has different characteristics and different applications.

DECLARATIVE OR SEMANTIC MEMORY

Declarative memory is mostly the stuff you know you know and can state explicitly, like facts, principles, or ideas.

Sometimes it's stuff you put into your closet deliberately (multiplication tables, for example), and sometimes it's material that you know despite not having made any conscious effort to retain it (everything I know about Britney Spears, for example).

EPISODIC MEMORY

Episodic memory is also a form of declarative memory, in that you can talk about it, but it's related to specific events or experiences you've had.

For example, you may be able to remember a lot of things about dogs—they are pets, they have four legs, they are furry, they eat dog food, Scooby-Doo is a dog, and so on.

But you also probably have episodic memories about specific dogs that you've known—your childhood dog, the neighbor's dog, or the scary dog that followed you to school when you were little.

STORYTELLING

Episodic memory refers specifically to our memory for things that have happened to us in our lives, but even when a particular story didn't happen to us personally, we seem to have a singular ability to remember stories.

At the beginning of their book *Made to Stick*, Chip and Dan Heath compare two passages. The first is an urban legend (a man meets a woman in a bar and wakes up later in a bathtub full of ice with a kidney missing), and the second is a paragraph about the return-on-investment rationale for non-profit organizations (or something like that).

A few years after reading the book, I can still remember several salient details from the urban legend and nothing at all about the second passage. There are multiple reasons why that's the case, but a big part of it is because the first passage is a *story*.

There are a few reasons why stories seem to stick in our memories:

- **We have a framework for stories.** There's a common framework for stories that we've all learned from the first stories we heard in childhood. Whether we realize it or not, in each culture there are common elements that we expect to hear when someone tells us a story. There's a beginning, middle, and end. There's the setup, the introduction of the players, and the environment. There's The Point of the story, which is usually pretty easy to recognize when it comes along. These are all shelves in our "how storytelling works" closet that give us places to store the information as we encounter it.

- **Stories are sequential.** If I tell you 10 random facts about tennis, you need to expend mental energy trying to organize those facts somehow, possibly grouping like items or using some other strategy. If I tell you the story of a particularly gripping tennis match with 10 significant events, then the sequence of events provides a lot of the organization for you. Additionally, there's an internal logic to events in stories (logically, dropping the carton of eggs can't happen *before* the trip to the grocery store in the story of having a bad day).

- **Stories have characters.** We have a lot of shelves to store information about people, their personalities, and their characteristics. If the story is about people we know, then we have all that background information to make remembering easier, and we have expectations about how they will behave. And if the character confounds your expectations by acting in a way that conflicts with your assumptions, that is surprising and novel and subsequently more memorable.

Which of the following would you be more interested in learning more about?

THIS?   OR THIS?

Insurance procedures

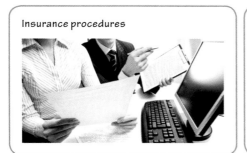

A story about Jim, a teen who was injured in a car accident, and how his family dealt with the aftermath

Steps to query a database

A story about Carla, the new employee who is the only one left in the office when the vice president calls down with an emergency request for updated reports

Human resources hiring best practices

A story about Marco, the replacement hiring manager in a company currently being sued for discriminatory hiring practices

CONDITIONED MEMORY

So you are cruising down the highway, and you glance in your rear view mirror and see a police car right behind you. Pop quiz—what do you do?

You slow down, right? Even if it becomes immediately apparent that the cop isn't the least bit interested in you, you've already dropped your speed, even if you weren't speeding in the first place.

What's happening there? Probably you didn't think to yourself, "Hmm, there seems to be a police officer behind me. Perhaps I should reduce my speed! I think I'll just gently let up on the gas pedal...easy does it..."

No, it was probably something more like, "WHOA!!" and you stomped your foot on the brake.

You see the stimulus of the police car, and you have what is a pretty much automatic reaction to what you see. This is what is referred to as a *conditioned response*.

Our conditioned responses are a form of implicit memory. Somewhere, stored in a part of your brain that you don't necessarily have explicit access to, there's a formula like this:

Everyone has reactions ingrained in their memory. Many are useful reactions acquired either through unconscious association or through deliberate practice:

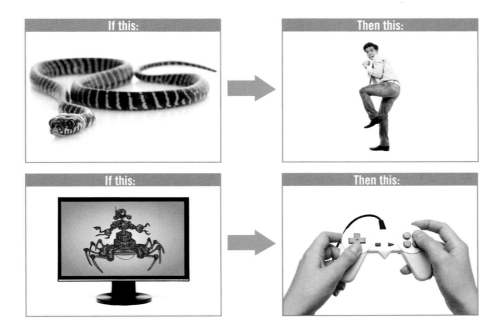

Some actions didn't need much effort to encode (like recoiling from a snake). We acquire others deliberately, through practice and repetition.

PROCEDURAL MEMORY

Procedural memory is our memory for how to *do* things. Specifically, it's our memory for how to do things that require a step-by-step process.

Some of the procedures you know are consciously learned, and you can explicitly state each step, but a lot of procedural memory is implicit.

Have you ever:

- Known how to get somewhere, but been unable to give somebody directions to that place?
- Gotten all the way home on your daily drive from work and realized that you have no memory of the drive itself?
- Been unable to remember a phone number or a PIN without tapping it out on the actual keypad?
- Thought you explained all the steps for a task to someone and then realized after it didn't work that you had neglected to mention some crucial details?

Those are all examples of utilizing something in your unconscious procedural memory. You use repeated practice of a procedure to make it become an unconscious habit. This is pretty important because it frees up your conscious attention to do other things.

Do you remember when you were first learning to drive? Everything required effort and attention.

Even if you were a pretty good student driver, you were still a bad driver, because you had to pay so much attention to everything until you acquired enough practice to start automating some of the steps. Attention is a finite resource, and new drivers spread it pretty thin. Fortunately, they start automating functions pretty quickly and can then allocate a bigger chunk of their attention to things like not crashing, or avoiding pedestrians.

When you've been driving for a while, you (presumably) have freed up a lot of your attention for other things besides the basic mechanics of driving, so you can then, for example, change the radio station while switching lanes and sing along at the same time. Of course, you may still be a bad driver years later, but that's probably due to other issues.

Automated procedural memory is related to the idea of *muscle memory*, which, despite the name, is still really a brain function. Muscle memory refers to your procedural memory for tasks you have learned so well through practice that you don't have to put *any* noticeable conscious effort toward them.

You get muscle memory through practice, and more practice, and even more practice (a process called *overlearning*). The biggest benefit of this is that you can perform the task without using up your conscious brain resources, freeing up those resources for other things.

It's frequently difficult to talk to others about these kinds of tasks, because you didn't learn them in a verbal, explicit way. You may know exactly how to adjust your golf swing to account for wind conditions, but you may not be able to explain it clearly to someone else. You can probably explain the overall motions, but not the subtleties (timing, how much pressure, the feel when you know it's correct).

FLASHBULB MEMORY

A few years ago, a freeway bridge near my home collapsed during rush hour, causing the death of about a dozen people and injuring over a hundred more. It was widely reported in the national media at the time.

I vividly remember where I was when I heard about it. I was in a meeting room at the office working on a conference proposal. The lights were dim, and one of the cleaning people came in and told me about the bridge. I remember what chair I was sitting in, all the details of the proposal I was working on, and which website I used to get more information about the incident.

This type of vivid memory for emotionally charged events is call *flashbulb memory*. It's common for people to be able to recollect exactly where they were when they heard about the September 11th terrorist attacks, for example.

So what is the cause of this type of memory, and what does it have to do with learning? (Not that staging a major newsworthy event is a practical way to encourage retention.)

Many believe that flashbulb memory developed as part of our brain's attempt to keep us alive.

If you survive a death-defying encounter, **you want to remember how you did it**. Remembering how you got away from the bear is a much higher survival priority than remembering where you left that rock. You can forget all sorts of day-to-day things without dying, but if you bump into a bear a second time, forgetting key information from your first encounter may get you killed.

Things you can forget and not die

Things that can kill you

Ordinarily, it takes time, effort, and repetition to get things into your long-term memory, but in emotionally charged circumstances the floodgates open and take in everything in the timeframe around the event. Sometimes it seems like time stands still.

One theory about why time seems to slow in an emergency is that you just remember so much more from those harrowing seconds than you do from the same amount of time in a normal circumstance. (Stetson 2007)

Even though I have never been personally harmed or threatened by an event like a bridge collapse or a terrorist attack, the heightened emotional charge of just hearing about the event seems to be enough to enhance my memory.

Even in less dire circumstances, emotion seems to have an impact on how much we remember. We will revisit this idea in later chapters and look at specific methods for using emotion to enhance retention.

REPETITION AND MEMORY

With a few exceptions, learning almost always requires practice and repetition. For some reason, these are some of the most neglected aspects of learning design. Ever heard a variation on this conversation?

FIRST SUPERVISOR: The staff is still throwing away the empty cartridges.

SECOND SUPERVISOR: But I *know* we told them not to. See, it's the third bullet point on slide 22 of the training presentation.

When you learn something new, connections are formed between neurons in your brain.

Like the paths that gradually develop when people repeatedly walk over the same ground, the connections that form in the brain are strengthened and reinforced whenever a learner re-encounters the material.

Connections that are reinforced become stronger and more durable. And, like a path that sees dwindling traffic, connections that aren't reinforced will usually fade or become irretrievable. Repetition and practice are necessary to successfully retain most learning for the long term.

Also, it's important for a learning designer to figure out how to have reinforcement without resorting to monotonous repetition. We know that multiple exposures to an idea improve the likelihood that the idea will be retained (well and good). *But* (and this is a big but) habituation tells us that people also tune out repetitive, unchanging things.

In the later design chapters, we look at how to reinforce an idea while avoiding tedious repetition.

MEMORIZATION: THE BLUNT FORCE SOLUTION

So if repetition is so critical, why is memorizing stuff such a pain in the butt? Should we just get tough and use lots and lots of repetition to grind that information into people's heads?

When I was in college, I took an architecture class. The professor was explaining about early church buildings. She explained that the people building the churches wanted to make the buildings as tall as possible, because they believed high ceilings enhanced churchgoers' religious feeling.

There were two different ways, the professor said, to make a building really tall: Use clever engineering to support the walls, or just make the walls really thick.

Using pure memorization to grind something into a learner's brain is the equivalent of building really thick walls—yes, it works, but it takes a lot of resources, and it's a clunky solution.

I will not just repeat things over and over.
I will not just repeat things over and over.

I will not just repeat things over and over.
I will not just repeat things over and over.

I will not just repeat things over and over.
I will not just repeat things over and over.

I will not just repeat things over and over.
I will not just repeat things over and over.

I will not just repeat things over and over.
I will not just repeat things over and over.

The biggest problem with memorization through repetition is that it frequently puts the information on just one shelf:

PIECES OF INFORMATION
Stuff I memorized

When you learn something by using it in context, you put it on multiple shelves and learn how to use that information in multiple contexts.

So basically, if you repeat something over and over, eventually you will wear a groove into your long-term memory, but there are some limitations to that approach.

- It's only on one shelf (basically the "stuff I memorized" shelf), which gives you only one place to look when you are trying to retrieve the information.
- You don't have experience using it in multiple contexts, so it's more difficult to take that information and transfer it to a variety of situations.
- You likely have sequential rather than random access to the information. If you learn something in a memorized sequence, then the context for that information is in that sequence, and your ability to retrieve it is also in that sequence. You probably have to tick through the list every time you need to retrieve something, which is much slower than being able to get directly to that item.

SUMMARY

- Memory relies on encoding and retrieval, so learning designers need to think about how the material gets into long-term memory, and also about what the learner can do to retrieve it later.
- Learners are besieged with a constant flow of input, and things need to be significant to the learner to attract their attention.
- People habituate to monotonous stimuli, so learning design needs to not fall into a repetitive drone.
- Working memory has its limits, and it's easy to overwhelm a new learner. Limit or chunk the flow of new information to make it more manageable.
- People hold items in working memory only as long as they need them for some purpose. Once that purpose is satisfied, they frequently forget the items. Asking your learners to do something with the information causes them to retain it longer and increases the likelihood that that information will be encoded into long-term memory.
- The organization of long-term memory has an impact on a learner's ability to retrieve material. The material will be easier to retrieve if it is grounded in a rich context and accessible in multiple ways (i.e., on multiple shelves).

HOW DO YOU GET THEIR ATTENTION?

(IN WHICH WE LEARN HOW TO TALK TO THE ELEPHANT)

IF THEY'RE NOT PAYING ATTENTION...

Do you remember the *Ooo, shiny!* learner?

Wired for distractions

Short, distributed attention

Thinks they multi-task, but really just switch focus a lot

In our current world of 24-hour-a-day distractions, this is pretty much everybody; we all have an excess of things that try to command our time and attention. And attention is pretty critical, right? If your learners aren't paying attention, then it doesn't matter what kind of learning experience you've created—they aren't getting much from it.

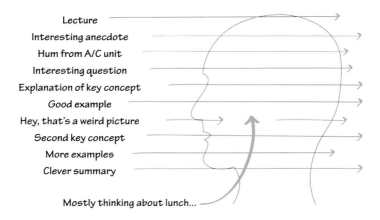

Lecture
Interesting anecdote
Hum from A/C unit
Interesting question
Explanation of key concept
Good example
Hey, that's a weird picture
Second key concept
More examples
Clever summary

Mostly thinking about lunch...

So how do you get your learner's attention? Well, to do that, you have to talk to the elephant.

TALK TO THE ELEPHANT

Jonathan Haidt, in his book *The Happiness Hypothesis*, talks about the brain being like a rider and an elephant:

> The rider is ... conscious, controlled thought. The elephant, in contrast, is everything else. The elephant includes the gut feelings, visceral reactions, emotions, and intuitions that comprise much of the automatic system.

He is talking about the idea that there are two separate parts of your brain that are in control—the conscious, verbal, thinking brain and the automatic, emotional, visceral brain.

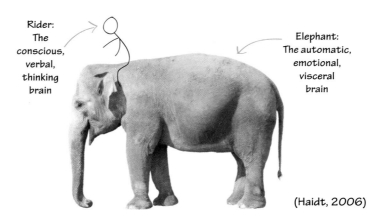

Rider:
The conscious, verbal, thinking brain

Elephant:
The automatic, emotional, visceral brain

(Haidt, 2006)

THE RIDER

The rider part of your brain is the rational, Mr. Spock, control-your-impulses, plan-for-the-future brain. Your rider tells you all sorts of useful things that you know will provide long-term benefit.

THE ELEPHANT

The elephant is your attracted-to-shiny-objects, what-the-hell, go-with-what-feels-right part of the brain. It's drawn to things that are novel, pleasurable, comfortable, or familiar.

The elephant *wants*, but the rider restrains that wanting. This is a really useful evolutionary advantage—the rider allows you to plan ahead and to sacrifice short-term wants for long-term gains.

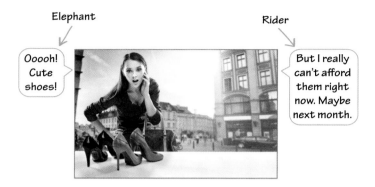

THE ELEPHANT IS BIGGER AND STRONGER

One of the challenges we all face, though, is that we have a tendency to over-estimate the rider's control. The rider is our conscious, verbal, thinking brain, and because it talks to us, we tend to think it's in control.

And sometimes that thought seems justified, because (again, sometimes) the elephant is willing and goes along with the rider pretty easily.

But other times, the elephant is going to do what it wants to, regardless of what the rider says.

And when the elephant and the rider are in serious conflict, guess who usually wins.

Exactly.

WHAT DOES THIS MEAN FOR YOUR LEARNERS?

Your learners have their own elephants:

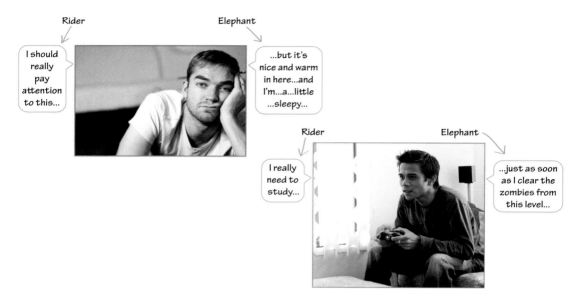

They look uncomfortably familiar, don't they? The important point is that if the elephant isn't engaged, the learner is going to have a heck of a time paying attention. But the rider can *force* the elephant to pay attention. We do it all the time. Any time you have forced yourself to complete a complicated homework assignment, fill out a tax return, or understand a legal document, you've been dragging your elephant along.

There's a cost to this, though. Dragging an elephant where it doesn't want to go is exhausting, cognitively speaking. We have to expend a lot of willpower to make it happen, and willpower gets used up pretty quickly.

In a study (Shiv 1999) participants were asked to remember either a two-digit number or a seven-digit number. They were subsequently offered a snack choice of either fruit salad or a piece of cake.

Approximately twice as many people chose cake in the seven-digit group as in the two-digit group.

This suggests that the cognitive resources of memory, focus, and control are finite. You *can* control the elephant, just not for very long. There have been a number of studies that suggest that self-control is a limited and exhaustible resource (Gailliot 2007; Vohs 2007). If your learners are having to force themselves to pay attention, there's a limit to how long they are going to be able to exert the control necessary to do so.

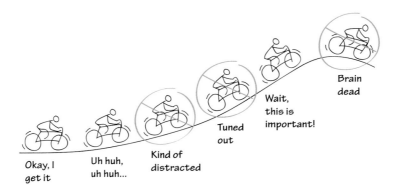

Okay, I get it

Uh huh, uh huh...

Kind of distracted

Tuned out

Wait, this is important!

Brain dead

Asking your learners to rely entirely on willpower and concentration is like asking the rider to drag the elephant uphill. (Note: Bicycling images are based on work I did at Allen Interactions and are used with their generous permission.)

Read the following paragraph:

> Right-of-way and yielding laws help traffic flow smoothly and safely. They are based on courtesy and common sense. Violation of these laws is a leading cause of traffic crashes. When two vehicles reach an intersection at the same time, and there is no traffic light or signal, the driver of the vehicle on the left must yield to the vehicle on the right.
>
> When two vehicles reach an intersection at the same time, and all-way stop signs or flashing red traffic lights control the intersection, the driver on the left must yield right of way to the driver on the right. (Minnesota Driver's Manual, p. 41)

How much effort did you have to put in to processing that text? It's not a particularly difficult concept, but your rider probably had to force your elephant to pay attention, and you had to put effort into translating the text into a visual so you could parse the information correctly.

Think about how that process *feels*. Unless you teach driver's ed or have a geeky fondness for driving regulations, it probably felt effortful and mildly unpleasant to have to force yourself to read and comprehend that passage. Just the kind of thing to make that chocolate cake look mighty appealing.

WE'D RATHER HAVE IT NOW

Behavioral economists study the concept of *hyperbolic discounting*, which is our tendency to prefer rewards that come sooner over rewards that happen later, even when the later reward is somewhat larger.

Think about your answer to the following questions:

    #1   Would you rather have $10 today or $11 tomorrow?

    #2   Would you rather have $10 today or $11 in a year?

    #3   Would you rather have $10 today or $1000 in a year?

When I've asked these questions of audiences in the past, I've gotten about a 50/50 split on question #1, everybody wanting the money today in question #2, and everybody willing to wait in question #3.

Basically, if the reward is big enough, we are willing to wait for it, but if it's not very big we aren't as interested.

If you think of this in learning terms, you have a similar transaction with your learners. You are asking them to pay attention to the lesson, and the reward for learning is getting to use what they've learned. Like money, attention is a resource that they can allocate (I don't think it's a coincidence that we talk about "paying" attention).

If they can use it immediately, it's not hard to pay attention, but if they can't use it immediately, it's much harder to remain attentive, even if the information is useful.

Think if it this way. If you had to rate your interest level in watching a video on printer repair, would you say that you were 1) Not interested at all 2) Somewhat interested or 3) Very interested?

I'm going to take a wild guess that you picked "1) Not interested at all." I could be wrong—you might have a long-standing interest in printer repair—but for most of us, this is not that interesting a topic.

Now imagine that you've got twenty minutes to print your loan application/grad school application/tax return/client proposal so you can get it in the mail by the deadline, and your printer is broken. How interested are you in videos of printer repair now?

Your level of interest didn't change because the video was different in the second scenario. It didn't magically become a wacky, entertaining, humorous video on printer repair. Engagement is often not property of the learning materials, but something that the learner brings when the materials are relevant or timely.

You can use this one of two ways. You can move the point of learning closer to the point of use (a just-in-time video that the learner watches only when they need it), or, if that's not possible, you can move the point of use closer to the point of learning, by using a scenario or problem for the learner to solve (more on that shortly).

ATTRACT THE ELEPHANT

If you can attract and engage the elephant (the visceral part of your learner's brain), there won't be nearly as much of a burden on the rider (the cognitive part of the brain). Think about really great learning experiences you've had. They are probably ones that have engaged your interests and curiosity on a visceral or emotional level. How we *feel* about something is a gauge of how important we think it is.

In the next section, we'll take a closer look at techniques for attracting the elephant, but all of them should be used with caution. The techniques that can be used effectively to attract the elephant can sometimes be *too* effective.

If the elements used to get the elephant's attention are not *intrinsic* to the learning subject matter and activities, then they can have a negative effect on learning and retention (Thalheimer 2004).

WAYS TO ENGAGE THE ELEPHANT

So how do you attract and engage the elephant?

- Tell it stories.
- Surprise it.
- Show it shiny things.
- Tell it all the other elephants are doing it.
- Leverage the elephant's habits.

TELL IT STORIES

Read the following story about a friend of mine:

> My friend Karen can't tell left from right. Just can't do it. When she really needs to know, she still holds up both hands to see which one forms the "L" for left.

As you might imagine, this is a bit of a problem while she's driving. She has a hard time following directions, and meeting another car at a four-way stop is practically cause for a panic attack.

She knows that the driver on the right gets to go first, but between the difficulty of figuring out which one is on the right and the inevitable second-guessing of that, she ends up doing a dance of start-stop-staaaart-stop-STOP until she winds up waving the other driver through regardless of who actually had the right of way.

I tried to convince her to put "Left" and "Right" signs in her car, but she said that was too embarrassing.

In the end, we glued a small lighthouse statue (a relic of some childhood vacation to the seashore) to the far right side of her dashboard. We refer to it as her "Right-light," and she always tells herself that if the other car is on the right-light side, then that car has the right of way.

Compare the experience of reading that passage to the experience of reading the passage about right-of-way and yielding laws earlier in this chapter. Which one required more effort? Was one passage easier to picture in your mind?

I think for most people, the story about Karen is probably easier to read and easier to visualize. It's also likely that you could re-tell Karen's story with reasonable accuracy, even after some time has elapsed.

PEOPLE LIKE STORIES

We like stories. We learn a lot from stories, and we seem to have a particularly good memory for them. A really well-told story can stick with us for years, even if we've only heard it once. In general, the elephant seems to be pretty willing to give stories an initial listen.

So what is it about stories that make them useful learning tools?

- **They go on existing shelves.** You already have a set of story shelves—you know how they work and what the parts of a story are. You know there's usually a main character, some kind of problem, and then a resolution of that problem. Some of this is culturally derived. If you are from the USA you might have a different story template than someone from Japan or someone from Malawi, but you already have shelves on which to put the story details.

- **There's a logical flow.** Stories usually involve sequenced events, and they frequently follow a chronological flow. You are more like to remember the sequence of crawl > walk > run than you are to remember the sequence of walk > run > crawl because there's a logical flow. Part of the promise of stories is that they will also have a logical flow involving cause and effect, and when you are recalling them, you can use that logic to recall what the events are. If someone retells the Karen story, they probably won't talk about the lighthouse on the dashboard before they talk about Karen's behavior at four-way stops.
- **Stories create suspense.** Whenever somebody starts telling you a story, there's an implied puzzle that you start trying to solve. What's the point of the story? Is it supposed to be funny? Is it going to be surprising? You start making predictions ("hmm...I know where this story is going...") or anticipating the purpose and outcome. The elephant likes puzzles (we'll talk more about this later in this chapter).
- **Stories aren't boring (we hope).** Of course there can be bad stories or tedious stories (let's face it, the Karen story isn't going to win any literary awards), but when someone starts telling a story, the implied promise is that there's an interesting reason for this story and therefore you should pay attention.

THE HERO

Another way to leverage storytelling in learning design is to make people the heroes of their own story.

A friend of mine who is a game designer says the purpose of game design is to *make the player feel smart*. Sebastian Deterding, a game researcher and academic, describes it this way:

> *Games satisfy one of our three innate psychological needs—namely, the need to experience competence, our ability to control and affect our environment, and to get better at it. (Deterding 2011)*

I think we have a similar responsibility when we design learning experiences, but I think our responsibility is to make the learner feel *capable*.

So how can your learners feel more capable?

- **Show them the before and after.** Your learner should be able to see how they will be different if they master the skills. What will they be able to do that they can't do now? Will they be more capable? Will they be able to handle problems that they can't right now? Will they have new tools to put in their professional toolbox? Show the learners what they can do and how they can get there.

Mild-mannered new hire

Help desk ninja

- **Give them real achievements.** Let them do meaningful things with the material while they are learning about it. Organize your content around those achievements. For example, which beginning Photoshop class would you rather take?

Photoshop for Beginners - Lesson Outline

Class A	Class B
Lesson 1: Working with layers	Lesson 1: How to create a swanky blog header
Lesson 2: Photo-editing tools	Lesson 2: How to make a so-so photo look amazing
Lesson 3: Working with filters and effects	Lesson 3: How to create an album cover
Lesson 4: Using the Pen tool	Lesson 4: How to remove your ex from your sister's wedding pictures

Which one is more likely to make the learner feel like they can actually accomplish something using the tool?

- **Create a first-person puzzle to solve.** Use a first-person story that runs through the whole learning experience. Say you're taking a sales course to teach you the features and benefits of a new product. How would you react to an opening slide that read "In this lesson, you will learn the features, benefits, and sales techniques for the Turboloader 3000" compared to one that showed a friendly agent in an open doorway, saying "The new Turboloader 3000 that just came in looks awesome! Hey, isn't your main client looking for a Turboloader? She's coming in today, isn't she?"

Suddenly, there's a *reason* to pay attention to the information. There's a goal, and time pressure, and a sense of urgency that "Learn about all the features and benefits of the Turboloader 3000" just doesn't instill.

URGENCY

As we discussed, it's much easier for learners to allocate attention if they can use what they are learning right away. Sometimes, that isn't possible, but you can simulate that by creating a sense of urgency. The feeling of immediacy and urgency is one of the biggest benefits you can get from using scenarios or stories in learning design.

Stephen Covey's 2x2 matrix of urgent versus important tasks highlights the fact that we frequently attend to the urgent rather than the important. Of course, we deal first with things that are both urgent *and* important, but after that, we tend to deal with the urgent (the email that just popped into the box) ahead of the important (the report due at the end of the week).

This is because the elephant is much more attuned to what feels urgent and immediate. Although learning to focus on the important may be a good life skill for individuals, it doesn't help you when designing learning that engages the elephant.

Remember the "things that can kill you" chart from Chapter 4? We are wired to pay attention to urgent things, because we evolved in an environment where "urgent" was frequently equivalent to "things that can kill you."

So which approach do you think would be more compelling for the elephant?

I wince now to think of when I was a new teacher and said things like "This is really important stuff" or "You'll be really glad you know this stuff later on." You can't capture the elephant's attention by just *asserting* that a topic is important. The rider may believe you when you say things like that, but the elephant knows better.

So what elements can you use to create a sense of urgency?

- **A compelling story.** Use classic storytelling elements to create a compelling scenario. Have a protagonist who is trying to accomplish a goal. Have an antagonist who is preventing the protagonist from accomplishing that goal. Have obstacles along the way that the protagonist must overcome. Have an inciting incident that sets up the drama of the story—a conflict that needs to be resolved. Make it so the protagonist needs to change and grow to overcome the obstacles.
- **Showing, not telling.** The elephant is pretty smart. It's not just going to take your word for it that something is important. It wants to SEE and FEEL the importance. This is one of the golden rules of fiction writing and movie-making: Avoid heavy-handed exposition, and instead use visuals, action, and dialogue.

- **Constraint of time or resources.** One indisputable way to raise the level of urgency is to create constraints. Give people time constraints or resource constraints and set them at a problem. Use caution here, however. Your learners will not appreciate having only five minutes to complete a 20-minute task; 15 to 18 minutes to complete a 20-minute task creates a sense of urgency. Five minutes to complete a 20-minute task creates pissed-off learners.

- **Immediacy.** In learning environments, we tend to focus on future consequences and outcomes, but the elephant is a creature of immediacy. Things that are going to happen in the future, regardless of how dire they are, are less compelling to the elephant than things that are happening RIGHT NOW. That's why "You may need to know these safety evacuation procedures" is far less compelling than "A fire just broke out on the 8th floor! Quick—what do you need to do first?"

- **Interesting dilemmas.** Give your learners interesting choices to make. Dilemmas capture attention if they are done well. The primary key to this is to not use right/wrong options. You can't wring much tension out of a right/wrong choice. Better options include choices between:

  - A good option and a very good option
  - Two bad options
  - Good, better, and best options
  - Two options that are each a mixture of good and bad, but in different ways.

  Well-designed games can provide fantastic examples of compelling dilemmas using constrained resources as pressure: Do you spend half your money to buy the railroad in Monopoly, knowing that it's a safer bet but will ultimately be worth less than holding out for the third green property? Either choice could be good or bad, depending on the circumstances.

- **Consequences, not feedback.** This goes back to the notion of show, don't tell, but uses actual consequences rather than feedback when people make choices in a learning scenario.

EMOTIONAL RESONANCE

Stories have an emotional resonance that can help us form opinions and make decisions. You don't just want people to learn things—you want them to be able to act on what they learn, and emotional context helps them do that.

For a long time, there was a myth of "rational decision-making"—that the best way to make decisions was to rationally weigh the pros and cons and not let messy emotions interfere.

Antonio Damasio, a behavioral neuroscientist, examined this idea by looking at patients who had brain damage in areas of the brain that support emotion. Rather than being clear and incisive decision-makers due to the absence of emotions, these patients found even simple decision-making to be extremely difficult. We seem to need an emotional "tug" to help us decide.

When we teach people facts that are stripped of broader context, we make it hard for those learners to act on that information. Of course, the necessity of emotional context varies depending on the subject matter. If I'm creating learning materials to teach bar staff how to use a cash register, I'm not going to be overly concerned with the emotional context. If I'm teaching that same group how to ensure that they aren't serving alcohol to underage or overly intoxicated drinkers, I'm going to be much more concerned about the emotional context.

Take a look at the following statement from a sales course:

> The sales commission on repeat sales is 10 percent.

This looks like the mother of all objective facts, right? Just another certainty to put on your list. But what happens if we add a little emotional context to that fact?

Facts are frequently meaningless to us until we see them in some kind of broader context that allows us to begin to make judgments about them.

Each picture on the previous page tells us a different story about how we should feel about a 10 percent sales commission. Maybe it's an awesome thing because industry standard is 4 percent. Maybe it's infuriating because the salesperson is used to a 30 percent commission.

We believe that there are "objective facts," but all valuable information has meaning only in a bigger context, and part of that context is emotional. If you don't use that context in learning design, your learner may gather facts, but they won't know how to *feel* about those facts. If they don't know how to feel about them, they won't know what to do with them.

SURPRISE THE ELEPHANT

One sure-fire way to get the elephant's attention is to surprise it.

UNEXPECTED REWARDS

When researchers test people using expected and unexpected rewards, there is greater activation of anticipation and reward structures in the brain when the reward is unexpected (Berns 2001). Basically, people have a much stronger response to unexpected rewards than they do to ones they know are coming.

For example, when I was growing up, I got a birthday card from my grandmother every year with a check for five dollars. Now this was always pleasing, because I love my grandmother and it was really sweet of her to do that, but the five dollars itself stopped being particularly exciting after about the age of twelve. There was always pleasure at the gesture from Grandma, but very little buzz around the money itself.

Compare that to the feeling you get when you are walking down the street and find five dollars lying on the ground, with no obvious owner in sight.

I don't know about you, but if I find five dollars lying on the ground, that's kind of awesome ("SCORE!"). And I probably keep a closer eye on the ground for a while after that happens.

The amount of money is the same in both examples, but the reaction is very different, due to the unexpectedness.

This tendency to react more strongly to unexpected rewards can be a valuable survival characteristic. Basically, if something is good, we want to remember that because we want *more*. And if something is bad, we want to remember that too, so we can avoid it in the future. But if something is *exactly the way we thought it would be*, there's really no reason to allocate mental resources to reinforcing that thought or idea.

Our apparently very-human reaction to an unexpected reward is a big part of why slot machines are so effective. They provide a variable reward schedule, which means we can't predict when we will get a win from the machine, so it's always a surprise when it happens. Unexpectedness is also part of our enjoyment of other entertainments, like sports or comedy.

Video games also do this well—we will be going along, collecting gold coins, when suddenly, after the 35th gold coin, we get the SUPER PLATINUM HAMMER OF DEATH. When something like that happens, we immediately start looking for the pattern. *What was I doing that caused that to happen? What can I do to make it happen again?*

In contrast, feedback in a lot of elearning is almost mind-numbingly consistent:

There are reasons why consistency can be helpful. The main one is reducing *cognitive load*. If an interface element (like a feedback box) is consistent, then I learn it once and don't have to allocate mental resources toward identifying its purpose after that. The problem with too much consistency is that I will start to ignore the box altogether pretty quickly.

If you are in a training class for a new computer system, and the instructor says, "OK, I'm going to start with the 37 main features of the system, with definitions of the functions for each feature," would you say "All right! Bring 'em on!" or would you say "Just kill me now..."?

But before you have a chance to say either, the instructor goes on to say, "Just kidding—we're just going to focus on the three most critical features. The rest of that stuff is in your manuals." Would you be more likely to pay attention to those three features at that point?

DISSONANCE

Another form of surprise happens when we bump into something that doesn't match our view of the world. Basically, there's no place in our closet for it.

Let's say you are walking down the street one day and you see a purple dog.

We've already talked about how you probably have a whole set of shelves in your closet for dogs. You probably have a pretty detailed mental model for dogs. But unless you have a traumatic dog-painting incident in your childhood, you probably don't have "purple" as part of your mental dog model.

So when you see the dog, you are comparing what you see with your existing formula for dogs (right size, right shape, right texture, right movement, right sounds—yep, it's a dog), but it's not the right color. There's enough there that *does* match your definition of dog, so you really don't question that, but you do stop at the color.

Now you have two opposing ideas in your head: "That's a purple dog" and "Dogs are not purple."

The term for this is *cognitive dissonance*—stuff just doesn't add up based on what you know about the world. You need to reconcile those two opposing viewpoints. How do you go about doing that? In the curious case of the dog, explanations could include:

- "Somebody spray-painted that poor dog."
- "I'm seeing things."
- "Maybe there really are purple dogs..."

In the last example, you are considering whether to reconcile and expand your mental model for dogs to include their being purple.

This is what some people will refer to as a "teachable moment." You get this nice element of friction that requires the learner to actively reconcile a disparate idea.

THE ELEPHANT IS A CURIOUS CREATURE

As my mother's first line of email tech support, I spend a lot of time on the AOL home page. AOL has a freakish ability to get me to follow article linkbait, frequently for things that I don't care about at all:

- Which '80s child star now has three wives?
- 8 reasons to avoid lip balm
- The surprising truth about fluorescent lights

I really don't *care* about any of these things, yet I find myself strangely compelled to click on them (I actually made up that list, but you get the idea). Whoever writes headlines for the AOL home page is a genius at tweaking my curiosity. It's shallow curiosity, but it still gets me to click on their link.

George Loewenstein, a professor of economics and psychology, describes curiosity as "arising when attention becomes focused on a gap in one's knowledge. Such information gaps produce the feeling of deprivation labeled *curiosity*. The curious individual is motivated to obtain the missing information to reduce or eliminate the feeling of deprivation."

The elephant is a curious creature, and if you can incite that curiosity you can get a lot of attention from the elephant. So how do you make the elephant curious?

- **Ask interesting questions.** If the question you are asking can be answered using a simple online search, it's not an interesting question. Interesting questions require your learner to interpret or apply the information, not just to recall it. Pure recall questions were never all that interesting, but in today's current technology- and information-rich world, they are just a waste of time.

- **Be mysterious.** Can you set up a mystery that needs to be solved? Can you make use of clever reveals? Can you start a science class by asking "Why does Saturn have rings? And why don't any of the other planets in our solar system have them?" (Cialdini 2005). How about starting a project-management class with a case study where the project failed spectacularly, and challenging the students to spot the reasons from the initial project documents? You can use a mystery as a framing device for instruction or as a puzzle for the students to solve.

- **Leave stuff out.** One of the ways the AOL headlines suck me in is by carefully leaving information out. It may turn out that the polygamist '80s child star is someone I barely remember from a show I never watched—or it might have been my absolute favorite actor from the show I watched religiously. The possibility is intriguing enough to pull me in. The reason I click is to close that knowledge gap.

  This is a tough idea for learning designers, because it's our job to make sure people have complete information and easy access to it. Leaving key information out is counterintuitive.

- **Be less helpful.** Dan Meyer, a math teacher and blogger (http://blog.mrmeyer .com), has a philosophy he describes as Be Less Helpful. I encourage you to check out his material for yourself, but my understanding of what he talks about is that we do our learners a disservice by making the problem too complete. By putting less information into the upfront presentation of the problem, we encourage our learners to work to fill in the gaps and learn strategies for approaching messy, ill-structured problems, instead of just learning how to plug the numbers into a formula. Framing and clarifying the problem becomes part of the learning experience.

Ask Interesting Questions

Take a look at this passage from nineteenth-century educator and writer Charlotte Mason:

Seeing that we are limited by the respect due to the personality of children we can allow ourselves but three educational instruments—the atmosphere of environment, the discipline of habit and the presentation of living ideas. Our motto is 'Education is an atmosphere, a discipline, a life.' When we say that education is an atmosphere we do not mean that a child should be isolated in what may be called a 'child environment' specially adapted and prepared, but that we should take into account the educational value of his natural home atmosphere both as regards persons and things and should let him live freely among his proper conditions. It stultifies a child to bring down his world to the 'child's' level.

Let's say you are teaching this passage to an education class. You want to ask questions to engage the students. You could ask "What are the three educational instruments espoused by Charlotte Mason?" or "What does Charlotte Mason mean when she says 'education is an atmosphere'?"

You *could* ask those questions, but those questions suck. They are purely information-based questions and can be answered by scraping content out of the passage. Instead, think about questions that require the learner to use and apply the content of the paragraph. For example:

- How could a modern educator "take into account the value of [a] natural home atmosphere"?
- Mason says it "stultifies a child to bring the world to the 'child's' level," but are there times when you have to do that?
- What do you think Mason would say about Internet usage restrictions in schools?

Ask questions that require learners to create something new, or form an opinion, or apply a concept, not questions that require the rote recitation of information.

TELL IT THAT ALL THE OTHER ELEPHANTS ARE DOING IT

The elephant is a social creature; one way to get the elephant's attention is to create a sense of social engagement. We pay more attention when there are other people involved.

In an experiment done by the MIT Media Lab (Okita 2008), people interacted with a virtual agent in a virtual reality environment. In one group, the test subjects believed they were interacting with another person in avatar form; in the other, the test subjects knew they were interacting with a computer in humanoid form. In both cases, the test subjects were interacting with the computer, which behaved identically in both conditions.

When people believed they were interacting with a live person, they showed more visible signs of paying attention, learned more, and did better on post-tests. The only variable was that the test subjects believed they were interacting with a real person. Again, we pay more attention when there are other people involved.

Social learning can take many forms. It can involve group projects or be less formal knowledge exchanges using social media. In traditional learning environments, the teacher was the source of all knowledge—information was essentially handed to the students—but today, students bring a lot of knowledge and experience to any learning circumstance, and it's wasteful to not take advantage of that.

There are some specific ways to leverage social interaction to engage the elephant, including collaboration, competition, and social proof.

COLLABORATION

When you use collaborative learning, a number of social influences act to get the elephant involved. Group activities require negotiation, support, social obligations, and other small-group dynamics that require the elephant to engage and pay attention.

Collaborative learning has other benefits in addition to getting the elephant's attention. For example, Philip Uri Treisman, of the University of California, Berkeley, tells a story about trying to improve the math performance of minority students (primarily black and Hispanic students). Treisman and his colleagues speculated about possible causes of low performance—maybe the students hadn't had the same academic preparation at disadvantaged schools, or lacked good family support, or hadn't learned good study habits.

But when they investigated by actually observing the students, they found that none of these assumptions were true. They found that the minority students studied diligently and had supportive environments.

The clue came when Treisman and his colleagues compared the minority students' study habits to those of the much more academically successful Asian students. The main difference they found between the two populations was that the minority students studied alone and the Asian students studied *together*.

The Asian students studied in groups, helped each other with problems, acted as resources for each other, and interacted socially around the subject matter. The minority students typically worked very hard but worked alone, studying in isolation.

When Treisman and his colleagues created a structure to allow the minority students to work with each other, they became much more successful, equaling and frequently outperforming the rest of the students.

SOCIAL PROOF

Robert Cialdini, in his classic book *Influence: The Psychology of Persuasion*, talks about the principle of social proof—basically, the tendency of people to view an activity as more worthwhile if other people are doing it.

If learners can see that other learners are engaged with the material, or if a group of students know that previous classes performed well, they are more likely to engage and perform better themselves.

When I taught semester-long undergraduate classes, I would sometimes have students do class presentations throughout the semester. The tone and quality of the first few presentations would set the bar for the rest of the semester.

In an online learning environment, being able to see who else has taken a class or what their level of participation was can influence the behavior of subsequent students.

COMPETITION

Competition is a problem.

Competition is a social mechanism that equals instant urgency. Athletes who are about to compete start showing the physiological signs of arousal (increased heart rate, hormone release, skin reaction) before the physical part of the game even begins.

There's no question that competition can be a useful way to get the elephant's attention, but there are a number of problems with it as a learning strategy:

- **Not everyone is competitive.** Some people really enjoy competition, but some people really dislike it or find it stressful. While a little bit of tension can improve learning by focusing attention, a lot of stress will detract from the learning experience. Additionally, research suggests that it's a bigger negative for students who don't do well with competition than it is a positive for students who do respond well.
- **Competition teaches learners how to win.** Some people might say, "What's wrong with teaching students how to win?" But a focus on winning can suck all the air out of the room. Basically, a focus on winning means learners are no longer focusing on the material. Winning becomes the main goal, not mastery of the material, or understanding, or how to use the material to accomplish things. All of those are relegated to the status of "things that will help me win" rather than being the goal itself. This is particularly problematic if the reward for winning is something extrinsic, like money or prizes.
- **Competition as motivation isn't a good long-term strategy.** It suggests to learners that things that aren't structured as a competition are less worthy of attention, and it devalues the subject matter.

Competition can grab the elephant's attention, but it should be used sparingly, if at all. It's probably fine to use a small competitive game to break up a learner experience for participants, but it shouldn't ever be used as the primary method for motivating learners.

SHOW THE ELEPHANT SHINY THINGS

There are a number of visual or tactile ways to attract the elephant's attention, including visual aids, humor, and rewards that elicit a visceral response.

USE VISUALS, BUT BE CAREFUL

The elephant is very visual, and the images you use make a difference.

For example, we know (from earlier in this chapter) that this block of text isn't very engaging:

> When two vehicles reach an intersection at the same time, and all-way stop signs or flashing red traffic lights control the intersection, the driver on the left must yield right of way to the driver on the right. (Minnesota Driver's Manual, p. 41)

It does get better when we use a visual:

If you're looking for an even more dynamic example, think of car-racing video games. Video games are particularly masterful at creating visuals that attract (and possibly distract) the elephant.

There are several good resources on creating visuals. Robin Williams's *The Non-Designer's Design Book* and Connie Malamed's *Visual Design Solutions* are particularly good. Those books can give you a lot of guidance for creating compelling visuals, but there are a few things you should keep in mind.

Know why you are adding a visual. Visuals can have a lot of different purposes in instructional material. It's useful to know why are you adding a graphic. Some of the reasons to use visuals include:

- Decoration—Sometimes it's just about making it pretty. Breaking up text or adding visual appeal both have their place. Don Norman's book *Emotional Design* discusses research suggesting that attractive things work better than unattractive ones—possibly due to the positive reaction they bring out in users—and it can be useful to provide visual rests in lengthy text passages.
  Despite that, decorative graphics are the shallowest type of instructional visual and should be used with some caution. There is research that suggests decorative graphics can distract learners from the main material (Thalheimer 2004).
  Also, whenever possible, avoid visual clichés. We've all seen that generic "hand-shaking" stock art image too many times already.
- Progression—Sometimes visuals can be much more effective than a text-only explanation for showing a process or steps in a procedure. Visuals can be particularly useful in showing progression over time.

- Conceptual metaphorical—Visuals can help explain a concept or a metaphor in a way that description alone can't. Infographics are specifically intended to make complicated information easier to process or understand.

Without a background in mathematics, data analysis, or similar fields that require spending lots of time with big numbers, most people have a hard time comprehending unfamiliar numeric-based data in any meaningful way. Visualization can help people understand how to process that information when they don't already have a set of shelves in their mental model.

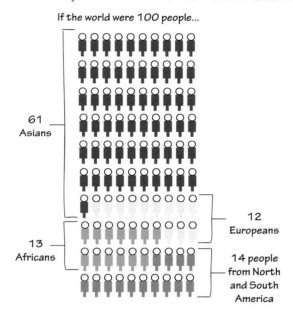

If the world were 100 people...

61 Asians

13 Africans

12 Europeans

14 people from North and South America

Visuals help distribute the load. Verbal and visual information seem to be processed differently by the brain, and as a result, effective use of both visual and verbal information helps keep learners from being overwhelmed by the material and gives them more ways to find the information again.

Anyone who's read a typical textbook knows it's got a *lot* more verbal information than visual information. To use our shelf metaphor, there's a whole lot of capacity on the visual side of the shelf that isn't being used. As I mentioned in Chapter 1, learning styles (e.g., visual, auditory, kinesthetic learners) aren't very useful, and part of the reason is that *everyone is a visual learner.* Unless someone has a vision or related impairment, they learn from visuals, and if we aren't taking advantage of that capacity, we are tying one hand behind our backs as learning designers.

Visuals can help build shelves. If your learners have small, general closets, and you have a lot of information to give them to put in those closets, visuals can be a good way to help them build a few shelves. Visual organizers can give learners a way to mentally parse the information they are receiving.

Visuals provide context. We've already talked about the critical importance of context, and visuals can provide a huge amount of context in a situation:

• Scenario context—You can spend a lot of time describing a scenario in words, or you can shortcut a lot of that wordiness using visuals. The setting where something takes place can provide a lot of information or triggers about a situation.

• Emotional context—Similarly, you can get a lot of emotional context from images. How much can you infer about each image below without having any words of explanation?

- Contextual triggers—One of the things we can do in a learning environment is to accustom our learners to certain behavior triggers.

  For example, I've recently been involved with a project where we want to educate people about "vampire" energy use—energy drawn from items like electronic devices that are plugged in but not currently being used. If you leave a cellphone charging overnight, the charger continues to draw power after the phone is fully charged, wasting energy. We want the learner to associate the sight of a plugged-in cellphone with the idea of potential wasted energy and then, consequently, with the action of unplugging fully charged phones.

Creating the visual association between the trigger and the action is an important part of encouraging the memory and the behavior.

LET THE ELEPHANT PLAY WITH STUFF

The elephant is also a tactile creature. When the elephant is difficult to corral, you can use hands-on methods to create engagement. You can use auditory, visual, and physical stimulation to attract attention. Buddhists sometimes talk about the "monkey mind," which is related to our mind's tendency to jump around and be easily distracted. One theory of neuroscience, neuroenergetic theory, proposes the idea that when we intensely use one area of our brains, that area gets depleted of resources such as blood glucose, which allows another area of the brain to grab center stage (Killeen 2013). So if you are trying to concentrate on your math homework at the coffee shop, the part of your brain that is reading calculus equations can get tired, and the part of your brain that was listening to the first date chit-chat from the couple at the next table can take over attention.

Using more fully tactile activities may help keep the monkey mind preoccupied, helping focus remain on the main task. For example, there is some research that suggests that doodling during a meeting or lecture can help people stay focused (Andrade 2009). Tactile activities that are directly related are presumably an even better option.

Things that you can taste, touch, hear, and smell also provide additional context that can act as memory triggers, and physical interaction can attract the elephant's attention by providing a different way to interact with material.

If the topic you are teaching has a hands-on component, then the learning should too.

MAKE WITH THE FUNNY

Let's just get this out of the way first: HUMOR IS SUBJECTIVE. Not everyone finds the same things funny. That makes using humor for learning a somewhat tricky business.

That said, if you are confident of your audience and confident that something is actually funny, then it can be used to good effect in engaging learners. Research studies have showed that students were better able to recall and complete funny sentences as opposed to neutral sentences, probably because the humor focuses learners' attention or because the humorous versions were more memorable (Schmidt 1994).

If you are trying to use humor, it's a really, really good idea to test it with your audience to make sure they agree with you about what's funny.

Some people think there's nothing funnier than a disgruntled kitten in a frog costume.

And some people really don't.

PRIZES! REWARDS! STUFF!

Another way to attract the elephant's attention is to let it know that there are prizes or rewards.

Oooh, is that for me??

But good use of rewards, like humor, can be a tricky business. At the most basic level, the idea is that if you reward a behavior, you increase the likelihood that behavior will occur, and if you punish a behavior, you decrease the likelihood that behavior will occur.

This can work if it's applied well in the right circumstances, but frequently it's not applied well.

WHAT'S GOOD ABOUT REWARDS

The best thing about these kinds of rewards is that they provide a certain immediacy, which helps keep the elephant engaged.

Let's say I want to learn financial literacy and investing for retirement, so I get a book on the topic. It tells me all sorts of useful things, but some of them I will have to wait until next quarter to implement (changing a payroll deduction), and some I won't be able to use potentially for years (how to best distribute my IRA income after retirement). But there isn't anything I can *do* with most of this information *right now*, which, as you might imagine, makes it a bit difficult to force myself to pay attention to it.

Compare that to learning about financial investing using a simulation game. You sit down, create an avatar, and start setting up your financial investment portfolio. You get to make decisions and play them through, skipping ahead years and decades at a time. You tweak and adjust your financial plan, and see how those decisions play out. You get to try completely different scenarios and see completely different outcomes.

The game scenario has a number of shiny advantages for attracting the elephant (feedback, risk, context, interesting and even fun challenges), but it also has the immediate rewards, punishments, and consequences that make it a compelling and "graspable" learning experience.

Don't get me wrong; books can have rewards too—it's not just the media that makes a difference. For an information junkie, the confirmations of already-gained knowledge and the new insights gained in books might provide a satisfying reward, but if you're not intrinsically motivated by the topic, you might need more specific challenges to accomplish, and more concrete rewards, in order to succeed in learning.

In the simulation example, there's something you can *do* immediately with the information you are learning. You don't have to work nearly as hard to persuade the elephant to pay attention, because the problem and questions are immediate.

WHAT'S BAD ABOUT REWARDS

But external rewards are a mixed bag. We've seen how they can be effective, but they can easily be misused. A good reward can be a moment of insight, a successful retirement portfolio in a simulation, or solving a puzzle. A bad reward is something that is extrinsic to the experience.

> **THE MAIN THING YOU NEED TO KNOW:** Extrinsic rewards can demotivate people.

You could hand out extrinsic rewards like candy ("Finish this course and get a gift card!"), but that's a shallow and ultimately ineffective way to motivate someone. It might work with pets, but it's a bad method for people. I've started referring to this as "the gift card effect." You know the drill—"We can't actually compensate you appropriately for this, but if you do it anyway, you can enjoy the equivalent of three pricey Coffee Beverages on us instead!" As a gesture of appreciation after the fact, these cards are fine. As a way to incentivize or motivate behavior, they are at best silly and at worst counterproductive.

Dan Ariely, a behavioral economist, did an experiment in which people were paid to make Lego shapes—a small sum for each shape they created. In one group, each Lego shape was displayed prominently when it was completed, and in the other each shape was broken back apart in front of the person and the pieces dumped back in the bins to be re-used (Ariely 2008).

Participants in the first group made significantly more shapes than people in the second, even though the financial rewards were exactly the same.

Similar effects are seen where people are asked to engage in an activity for the sake of that activity, rather than for financial payment or other extrinsic reward. Once you start paying people, it becomes work and can have a negative effect on performance and motivation. For example, kids who are rewarded for drawing pictures draw *less* than when it is a voluntary activity. It becomes work, or an obligation, when there's compensation involved. The emphasis can very quickly shift from the activity to the rewards (Kohn 1993).

Two excellent books on this topic are *Drive,* by Daniel Pink, and *Punished by Rewards,* by Alfie Kohn.

MAKING REWARDS MORE INTRINSIC

Rewards can be great motivators if they are intrinsic. Intrinsic rewards can take many forms, including (but not limited to) the satisfaction provided by the activity itself, the pleasure in a new capability, and the anticipation of being able to use new skills.

The common thread of all successful intrinsic rewards is that they need to be genuinely useful or satisfying to the learner. For example, we already talked about organizing a learning experience around real achievements:

Photoshop for Beginners
- Lesson 1: How to create a swanky blog header
- Lesson 2: How to make a so-so photo look amazing
- Lesson 3: How to create an album cover
- Lesson 4: How to remove your ex from your sister's wedding pictures

This learning experience has intrinsic rewards built right in, in the form of quantifiable and satisfying accomplishments. You can also consider how you would reward the different accomplishments. For example, you could give a big gold star and 1000 experience points to learners for each item they accomplish, but that's a pretty extrinsic type of reward.

A better reward might be to create an online gallery where learners could display the results of their accomplishments. This form of reward would be much closer to the intrinsic nature of the task.

YOU DON'T GET TO DECIDE

There's one catch to designing for intrinsic rewards:

You don't get to decide what's intrinsic to the learner.

Any form of intrinsic reward has to be flexible and has to ensure that the learner has at least some control. If there aren't options and autonomy for the learners, then you are just guessing what is meaningful to them. Sometimes you may guess right (and the likelihood of that goes up when you really know your learner well), but ultimately you want to give the learner as much control as possible in letting them decide what's meaningful.

I've heard the argument that learners don't know what they don't know, and that they need guidance and directions. This can be a justification for less autonomy in an environment, but there are always ways to give options to even the most novice learners.

Some ways you can give learners autonomy:

- Let them help determine what's learned.
- Let them choose where to start, or in what order to approach the material.
- Have them make decisions about what assignments or projects they do.
- Have them bring their own questions, projects, or problems to the table, and focus the learning experience around addressing or solving those challenges.

If you genuinely can't give learners any autonomy, then stay away from any kind of rewards as a way to drive attention. There's no such thing as mandatory fun, after all.

SUMMARY

- If you want to get and maintain your learners' attention, you need to talk to the emotional, visceral brain (elephant) as well as to the conscious, verbal brain (rider).
- *Attracting* attention is not the same thing as *maintaining* attention. Make sure the device you use to attract attention is intrinsic to the material being learned. If it's not, it may actually be distracting and negatively impact learning.
- Attention is much easier for learners when they are going to be able to use the material right away. If possible, have the point of learning be close to the point of use (just-in-time learning). When that's not possible, use scenarios or problem-solving to create the feeling of immediate usefulness.

- Some ways to attract your learners' attention include stories, emotional resonance, urgency, surprise, and interesting puzzles.
- Social interaction and visual cues will go a long way to attracting and maintaining attention.
- Devices like competition and extrinsic rewards will attract your learners' attention, but they will almost certainly distract them from the real goal and have a negative impact on their intrinsic motivation. They are best avoided unless used very carefully.
- Intrinsic rewards almost always require learner autonomy or choice to be effective.

REFERENCES

Andrade, Jackie. 2009. "What Does Doodling Do?" *Applied Cognitive Psychology* (January 2010). 24 (1): 100-106.

Ariely, Dan, Emir Kamenica, and Dražen Prelec. 2008. "Man's Search for Meaning: The Case of Legos." *Journal of Economic Behavior & Organization* 67: 671–677.

Bean, Cammy. 2011. "Avoiding the Trap of Clicky-Clicky Bling-Bling." *eLearn Magazine*, June. http://elearnmag.acm.org/featured.cfm?aid=1999745.

Berns, Gregory S., Samuel M. Mcclure, and P. Read Montague. 2001. "Predictability Modulates Human Brain Response to Reward." *Journal of Neuroscience* 21 (April).

Cialdini, Robert. 2005. "What's the Best Secret Device for Engaging Student Interest? The Answer Is in the Title." *Journal of Social and Clinical Psychology* 24 (1): 22–29.

Deterding, Sebastian. 2011. "A Quick Buck by Copy and Paste," posted by *Gamification Research Network*. http://gamification-research. org/2011/09/a-quick-buck-by-copy-and-paste.

Gailliot, M.T., R.F. Baumeister, C.N. DeWall, J.K. Maner, E.A. Plant, D.M. Tice, L.E. Brewer, and B.J. Schmeichel. 2007. "Self-Control Relies on Glucose as a Limited Energy Source: Willpower Is More Than a Metaphor." *Journal of Personality and Social Psychology* 92: 325–336.

Haidt, Jonathan. 2006. *The Happiness Hypothesis: Finding Modern Truth in Ancient Wisdom*. New York: Basic Books.

Jabr, Ferris. 2010. "The Psychology of Competition: Meeting Your Match." *Scientific American Mind* Nov/Dec: 42–45.

Killeen, Peter R. 2013. "Absent Without Leave: A Neuroenergetic Theory of Mind Wandering." *Frontiers in Psychology*. 4: 373.

Kohn, Alfie. 1993. *Punished by Rewards: The Trouble with Gold Stars, Incentive Plans, A's, Praise, and Other Bribes.* Boston: Houghton Mifflin.

Loewenstein, G. 1994. "The Psychology of Curiosity: A Review and Reinterpretation." *Psychological Bulletin* 116(1): 75–98. Found via Stephen Anderson's excellent article on Johnny Holland.

Mason, Charlotte. 1923. "Three Instruments of Education." *Charlotte Mason's Original Homeschooling Series* 6: 94. Copyrighted 2002–2003 by Ambleside Online.

Minnesota Driver's Manual. www.dps.state.mn.us/dvs/DLTraining/DLManual/DLManual.htm.

Okita, S.Y., J. Bailenson, and D.L. Schwartz. 2008. "Mere Belief of Social Action Improves Complex Learning." *Proceedings of the 8th International Conference for the Learning Sciences.*

Pink, Daniel. 2009. *Drive: The Surprising Truth About What Motivates Us.* New York: Riverhead Books (Penguin).

Schmidt, S.R. 1994. "Effects of Humor on Sentence Memory." *Journal of Experimental Psychology: Learning, Memory, and Cognition* 20: 953–967.

Shiv, B. and A. Fedorikhin. 1999. "Heart and Mind in Conflict: The Interplay of Affect and Cognition in Consumer Decision Making." *Journal of Consumer Research* 26 (December): 278–282.

Thalheimer, W. 2004 (November). "Bells, Whistles, Neon, and Purple Prose: When Interesting Words, Sounds, and Visuals Hurt Learning and Performance—A Review of the Seductive-Augmentation Research." www.work-learning.com/seductive_ augmentations.htm.

Treisman, Philip Uri. 1990. "Academic Perestroika: Teaching, Learning, and the Faculty's Role in Turbulent Times." From an edited transcript of his lecture of the same name, delivered March 8, 1990, at California State University, San Bernardino. www2.ed.gov/about/offices/list/ope/fipse/perestroika.html.

Vohs, Kathleen D. and R. J. Faber. 2007. "Spent Resources: Self-Regulatory Resource Availability Affects Impulse Buying." *Journal of Consumer Research* (March).

DESIGN FOR KNOWLEDGE

(IN WHICH WE LEARN TO NOT HAND OUT MITTENS IN SUMMERTIME AND TO LET LEARNERS HOLD THE MAP)

In this chapter, we will focus on a few basic challenges we face when designing a system to convey knowledge:

- Will your learners remember?
- Do the learners understand?
- How much guidance do you give learners?

We'll also take a look at a process for designing learning solutions.

WILL THEY REMEMBER?

Let's look at a few of the many ways to make content more memorable.

> **THINK ABOUT SHELVES:** One way to embed content more firmly in memory is to already have some shelves the learner can use to store the information.

HAVE LEARNERS CONSIDER WHAT THEY ALREADY KNOW

A lot of times learners already have some knowledge of a topic, and you can draw that out. For example, if you are teaching a group of people how to write good job descriptions, you can ask the group to tell you everything they think needs to go into a job description, and then work from that list.

Collecting such a list from learners accomplishes two key things. It gets them to dust off and look at their existing shelves for job descriptions, and it has them think actively about what the shelves should be for writing job descriptions.

After you've generated the list, you can edit it, adding missing elements or removing items as you go. If you need to remove something, that becomes an active process ("Here's why this isn't necessary…").

Instead of trying to just remember what you said, learners are actively stimulating and adapting their existing model.

Whenever you want to tell your learners something, first ask yourself if there's any way they can tell *you* instead.

HAVE LEARNERS CONSTRUCT THEIR OWN FRAMEWORK OF SHELVES

Metacognition is a term that loosely means "thinking about thinking." Among other things, it means being aware of how you are learning.

You can have students take an active role in their own metacognition. For example, problem-based learning is a teaching method originally developed in medical schools to supplement or replace pure information-delivery teaching methods (Barrows 1996).

Traditionally, medical students, being a motivated bunch, learned information really well but couldn't always apply it. Problem-based learning was intended to help them better apply the information they'd learned.

An example of problem-based learning might work roughly like this: A facilitator gives a small group of students a case ("A 38-year-old female with chest pains and dizziness"), and the students proceed to diagnose the patient. While the students work through the case, they keep track of a few categories on a whiteboard.

Facts	Ideas	Learning Issues
What do we know?	What are our hypotheses?	What are our knowledge gaps?

The whiteboard is a way the students can keep an explicit list of what they know, what they think, and where they don't know enough. Frequently, students are given the responsibility of investigating the areas on the learning issues list and bringing the information back to the group. This can vary depending on how a particular problem-based learning lesson is designed, but one of the fundamental ideas is to make the students aware of their own knowledge and, even more importantly, of the *gaps* in their knowledge.

Another way to have your learner be more aware of their own learning is to give learners an inventory of the content, and have them rate their level of comfort with each topic. As they go, they can adjust their ratings, either as they get more comfortable or as they realize they don't know as much as they thought they did. While these ratings don't mean the learners have actual proficiency, it does involve them in tracking their own understanding and focuses them on eliminating gaps.

MAKE IT STICKY

Imagine you work taking the ticket stubs in a movie theater. You rip tickets for hundreds of people every day. At the end of the day, how many of those people do you think you remember?

You are only going to remember the people who really stood out, right? This isn't a failing of your memory—it's how things are supposed to work. If something isn't significant, important, or unusual, why would we want to remember it?

The problem occurs when we can't hold onto things that we *want* to remember.

In Chapter 4, we talked about how working memory has a really short duration, and you forget most of the things you have in working memory unless you are actively trying to keep them there through rehearsal or because they are significant or memorable.

If something doesn't stand out for some reason, there's a good chance it will just pass through without leaving much of a mark, like water through a pipe.

This can be particularly true if it is information the learner already thinks they know or understand—why would you pay attention to something you already know?

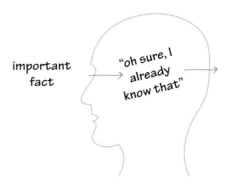

We seem to be particularly susceptible to this one—the one where we already think we know the material—which is problematic for two reasons. First, it may be a problem because we may not know it *enough*. In Chapter 4, we looked at how it's more difficult to *recall* something than it is to just *recognize* it. We may think we can recall, when all we can do is recognize. The second possible reason that this is a problem is because we may only *think* we understand; we may actually have misconceptions or incomplete understandings that we don't realize we have.

In a research study (Muller 2008) that looked at using videos to teach science concepts, students who received only clear, well-explained visual explanations of physics concepts rated the videos highly, saying that they were indeed clear and easy to understand.

Another group of students were first shown videos that had explanations or dialogues between two characters discussing common misconceptions about physics principles, and then they (the students, not the characters) were given the explanation of those principles.

The group that heard the discussions of the misconceptions rated the videos *less* easy to understand—they were more confused than if they had received only the explanation. But the second group did much better on the post-test and showed significantly more improvement than the first group.

So even though the second group felt *more confused*, they actually understood much better. Arguably, this has to do with them having their assumptions confronted and having to actively reconcile misconceptions.

CREATE FRICTION

Learning is messy, and interacting with and resolving that messiness can help embed the information into long-term memory. We want learners to engage with the material.

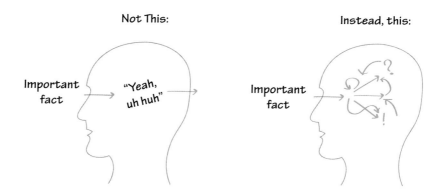

Passive experiences like lectures or page-turner elearning courses, where the information is just channeled to the learner, can also flow smoothly right *by* the learner. If the learner is actively engaging with or interested in the material, then a passive information-delivery system can still be an effective tool. But if your learner is even mildly disengaged, this same method probably won't accomplish much. Creating opportunities to interact with the material can make a lesson even more engaging for your motivated learners.

If you don't want the material to flow smoothly past (or around) your learners, then you want to provide a little friction—something that requires learners to chew on the material, cognitively speaking. This is also sometimes referred to as *desirable difficulty.*

John Sweller, a prominent educational psychologist, uses the term *cognitive load* to describe how much information someone can process at any one time (Sweller 1988). He talks about intrinsic, extraneous, and germane cognitive load.

If you were taking an online class studying dinosaur biology, then:

- The *intrinsic* cognitive load would be the specific information about dinosaurs that you are trying to learn.
- The *extraneous* cognitive load would be the annoying web interface for the online course that doesn't quite fit right on your screen. It requires effort and attention, without adding to your knowledge of dinosaurs.
- The *germane* cognitive load could be a design-your-own-dinosaur activity that the instructor uses to help you interact with the concepts you are learning. The activity isn't necessarily the intrinsic content, but it provides some friction to help you interact with the intrinsic content.

I often describe one of the main functions of learning design as "the ruthless management of cognitive load." You want to figure out ways to increase friction (germane cognitive load) while minimizing extraneous cognitive load.

We've already talked about a number of ways to make the learning experience more interactive, which is the main way you can add friction, but let's take a look at a few more.

SHOW, DON'T TELL

Cathy Moore, an outstanding elearning designer (www.cathy-moore.com), has a checklist of items that she uses to evaluate whether a learning experience is action-oriented or more of an info dump. One of the criteria she looks at is whether the course **shows** or **tells**:

> *...feedback that shows learners what happens as a result of their choice; learners draw conclusions from the result.*

> *vs.*

> *...feedback that explicitly tells learners "correct" or "incorrect"; learners aren't allowed to draw conclusions.*

> *(Moore 2011)*

One of the reasons this is important is that *telling* is smooth but *showing* has friction: It requires learners to make some of their own connections to interpret what's going on.

Showing rather than telling is a big theme in fiction writing:

> *The difference is that in telling there's absolutely no role for the viewer or the reader to put anything together. In showing, the viewer has a chance to put stuff together themselves and to be active in the story.*
>
> *It's so much more engaging as an audience member if I am left to put stuff together myself and not have it all assembled for me and handed to me...*
>
> *You need to give your readers stuff to do. Give them a way to be an active participant, and by allowing them to draw conclusions based on little clues that you leave, you engage them in the story and they become part of it.*
>
> —*Lani Diane Rich*, StoryWonk Daily

Arguably, reading fiction is not interactive in the same way as a classroom activity or an elearning simulation, but even how something is written can allow the learner a more or a less active role.

There's other research that bears this out. In one study (Kuperberg 2006), subjects were shown sentence pairs. Some of the sentence pairs went together very easily (x obviously causes y), some required some interpretation to see the connection, and some were unrelated. One of the (somewhat violent) examples from the study is:

> *Main sentence: "The next day his body was covered in bruises."*

That sentence was preceded by one of these statements:

> *"Joey's brother punched him again and again."*
> *(Highly causally related—x obviously caused y.)*
>
> *"Joey's brother became furiously angry with him."*
> *(Intermediately causally related—you've got to read between the lines a little.)*
>
> *"Joey went to a neighbor's house to play." (Pretty much unrelated.)*

The subjects spent the most time on the middle sentences—they were related but forced the subjects to connect some dots to see the connection. The study saw a greater degree of brain activation in many areas for those sentences, and they were better remembered later.

So if people have to make the connections themselves, it's likely they'll remember more later.

Ways to show rather than tell

Tell	Show
"In this lecture, we'll discuss the five primary ways that criminals can use the stock exchange to launder money..."	"You are an embezzler, and you need to hide $800,000 in illicit funds. What's the first thing you can do to launder the money? Choose one of the options below..."
"You chose to offer the customer the XYZ model of refrigerator, but that model is too expensive for this customer. The ABC model would have been a better choice."	"The customer shrugs and says 'I'll think about it' before he wanders off in the direction of the dishwashers. Try the scenario again, and see if you can be more successful with a different model."
Driver's Ed teacher: "Here are the rules for when you encounter a school bus. First, if the light is flashing..."	Driver's Ed teacher: "So what do you think are the biggest concerns with a stopped school bus? What would people be worried about? Right—they'd be worried about kids exiting and crossing the street..."
"A highly irate woman comes into the restaurant..."	"A 50-ish woman in a business suit slams into the restaurant and charges up to you. 'Look!' she says, 'I come in here ALL THE TIME, and I am not used to being treated like this...'"
"One of the biggest issues with project management is scope creep. Let's list some ways that scope creep can happen..."	"OK, class, you all had update meetings with your project clients this week. What issues came up? Were there any problems with the deliverables you had due this week?"

For the following three scenarios, how could you change them from tell to show? Consider each scenario again before reading the design solution below (which is of course just one of many possible solutions).

SCENARIO 1: PRESENTING A DIET

You hear a diet presented this way:

> Here's an example of a balanced, 2000-calorie-a-day diet. It's been carefully balanced to contain 55% carbohydrates, 15% protein, and 30% fat.

How could you change this from *tell* to *show*?

—TAKE A MOMENT TO CONSIDER WHAT YOU WOULD DO BEFORE MOVING ON—

Design Solution 1

One solution is to involve the person more directly:

> You need to create a balanced, 2000-calorie diet that is approximately 55% carbohydrates, 15% protein, and 30% fat. Choose foods from each of the categories to create your meal plan for the day. Make sure you also select a quantity. When you're done, I'll give the nutritional information for the food lists, and you can see how close you came and what you would need to adjust to meet the requirements. ■

SCENARIO 2: CALCULATING COMPENSATION

When determining employee compensation levels, you want to take years of experience, qualifications, and the pay rate of comparable employees into consideration.

How could you change this from *tell* to *show*?

—TAKE A MOMENT TO CONSIDER WHAT YOU WOULD DO BEFORE MOVING ON—

Design Solution 2

> Take a look at Jane's qualifications and company history. She's being pro-moted into your department. How much are you going to pay her? Here's the same information for the other four members of your department, plus the salary histories for each employee. ■

SCENARIO 3: LEARNING SOFTWARE

The red highlight shows you where to click to open the customer record. Click the highlighted area, and then click Next to move to the next screen.

How could you change this from *tell* to *show*?

—TAKE A MOMENT TO CONSIDER WHAT YOU WOULD DO BEFORE MOVING ON—

Design Solution 3

> Where on this screen do you think you would need to click to open the customer record? If you get stuck, you can consult the Help function or request a hint. ■

SOCIAL INTERACTION

Another way to add some friction to learning is to use interpersonal interaction. Each learner is going to bring their own perspectives and experience to the table, and sharing and debating can be good ways to engage with a topic.

Discussion topics can facilitate this ("discuss the consequences of sexual harassment complaints in the broader organization"), but you generally get better results if you give groups a more concrete purpose. They could:

- Create something
- Work together to teach something to the rest of the class
- Argue different sides of a debate
- Investigate and report back (e.g., find three good examples, or a bad example, and bring them back to the class)

Let's say you are teaching a group how to write a good help-wanted advertisement. You could employ small group interaction by having the learners:

- Work together to create a job advertisement for a position
- Research different aspects of equal employment guidelines and present that information back to the class
- Rank-order five advertisements you've given them, from best to worst, and why
- Identify all the problems with some bad job listings you provide
- Research online and find three good job listings to bring to the class, with the criteria they used

Requiring all of these activities would clearly be overkill (and of course these suggestions are not exhaustive), but social interaction can be a good source of learning friction, so you want a variety of ways to include and leverage that.

HELPING YOUR LEARNERS UNDERSTAND

You don't just want your learners to remember—you also want them to *understand*.

The first part of helping ensure that your learners will understand what you want to teach them is to start with the right content.

The right content is:

- Less than you think it is
- Enough detail but no more
- Relevant to the learners
- Stuff that can fit in their closet, with some expansion or rearranging

Remember that one of your main functions as a learning designer is "the ruth-less management of cognitive load." Part of this is ensuring that learners aren't overwhelmed by the amount of content.

THE RIGHT AMOUNT OF CONTENT

What's the right amount of content for your learners? Probably less than you think it should be. Working memory has a pretty limited capacity (we talked about this in Chapter 4), and it's highly likely that you'll want to communicate more content than your learners are in a position to take in.

It might help to think about it this way:

You can keep handing material to your learners, but you can't make them carry it around. Look closely at the material you want to communicate, and focus on the parts that are most relevant to learners. Anything else, you may need to provide as a resource for them later. Be ruthless about including only what's really necessary.

For example, let's say you want to teach somebody who has never baked how to make an apple pie. When it comes time to give instructions about putting on the top crust, don't digress into alternate explanations of how you can also do a lattice top or a streusel, or a side discussion about different theories of steam vents, or a lengthy explanation about the way the proteins react if you overwork the gluten in the dough.

If someone is new to baking, stick with one way to do things. You can always elaborate later.

It's really easy to overestimate the right level of detail for your audience. The best way to know how much is too much is to try it out and see how they do.

The Average Attention Span

Every once in a while I see some statement about learners' average attention spans. Maybe you've seen proclamations that "the average adult attention span is no more than 10 minutes" or 15 minutes, or 45 minutes, or...

If you think about it, this is just silly.

There's a movie theater near my house that shows a back-to-back marathon of all *The Lord of the Rings* movies every holiday season, and it's really well attended. And it's the extended editions of each movie.

That's over eleven hours of movies, people. That's the attention span of that audience—over eleven hours.

Aside from the constraints of hunger, fatigue, and bathroom breaks, there's really no limit on someone's potential attention span. What may be much more limited is the length of time someone can *force themselves* to pay attention. Remember the elephant? If the elephant is happily romping with the hobbits, then attention is easy, but if you are asking your learners to corral the elephant, then the clock is probably ticking. You might be lucky to get 10 minutes from someone if you are explaining the procedures for their health savings account.

It's still not really plausible to put a number on it, though. It depends on too many variables—how much sleep that person got, whether they ate breakfast, if they are interested or motivated about the topic, whether the presentation is dynamic or monotone. There's really no way to say.

The important part of trying it out is to *start lean* and test your content with your audiences to see where the holes are. Start with as little as you can get away with. If it's not enough, you'll find out quickly because the learner will be confused or will have questions. The gaps will bubble up like leaks in a submerged air mattress. If you start with too much, it'll be harder to identify those excesses. You might be able to tell where you are really overloading your learners, but a lot of the little extras might not be immediately visible as extraneous.

We've already talked about *getting* learners' attention, but there are also things you can do as a learning designer to *keep* learners interested:

- **Be entertaining.** This works, but can frequently be the most difficult to pull off (particularly if you aren't naturally the life of the party). Still, there's a lot to be learned from entertainment media (movies, TV, games, etc.) about being more entertaining. There are also some good resources on being more engaging. Some recommendations include *Made to Stick,* by Chip and Dan Heath; *Resonate,* by Nancy Duarte; and *Presentation Zen,* by Garr Reynolds.
- **Ask questions.** It's a lot harder to disengage if you have to think about how to respond.
- **Change it up.** Mix together presentation and activities and types of media.
- **Have them interact.** It's a lot of pressure on you to provide all the interaction; let learners interact with each other.
- **Have them make stuff.** Don't just have activities, have activities where they make stuff.

MISCONCEPTIONS

Another issue you'll have to contend with is learners' misconceptions. There are a couple of strategies that can help prevent misconceptions.

First, as we've looked at in previous chapters, you want to make sure you know what your learners are understanding. Having good feedback loops, where you get learners to answer questions, give examples, and explain an idea or concept back to you, are all ways to do this.

Another strategy is using *examples* and *counter-examples*. If you ever read *Highlights* magazine in your dentist's waiting room as a child, you might remember the characters Goofus and Gallant. Goofus always got it wrong, while Gallant always got it right. Goofus would take the last piece of fruit for himself, while Gallant would generously share his orange. The Goofus and Gallant comics were classic examples of matching an example with a non- or counter-example.

This technique can be particularly effective in preventing misconceptions. For example, when I learned about writing survey questions in graduate school, the professor had us look at terrible survey questions to learn how to write good ones.

Let's say you want to teach someone about writing good true–false questions. You could explain some of the guidelines:

Guidelines for Good True/False Questions

Ask about only one thing at a time.

Test for knowledge, not memorization.

Avoid using qualifying words.

That's OK, but you'd probably want to elaborate with some examples:

Guidelines for Good True/False Questions	Example
Ask about only one thing at a time.	The guideline for the minimum following distance while driving is the 4-second rule. (True or False)
Test for knowledge, not memorization.	A 130-lb woman can consume three 12-oz beers in an hour and feel confident she has a blood alcohol content within legal guidelines for driving. (True or False)
Avoid using qualifying words.	When you hear an emergency siren while driving, you should pull over. (True or False)

OK, so the examples *help*, but what if we add counter-examples?

Guidelines for Good True/False Questions	Good Example	Bad Example
Ask about only one thing at a time.	The guideline for the minimum following distance while driving is the 4-second rule. (True or False)	Safe following distance while driving can be measured using the 4-second rule or by having two car lengths between you and the other vehicle. (True or False)
Test for knowledge, not memorization.	A 130-lb woman can consume three 12-oz beers in an hour and feel confident she has a blood alcohol content within legal guidelines for driving. (True or False)	The formula for determining blood alcohol content is %BAC = (A x 5.14/W x r) - .015 x H. (True or False)
Avoid using qualifying words.	When you hear an emergency siren while driving, you should pull over. (True or False)	When you hear an emergency siren while driving, you should always pull over immediately. (True or False)

How much do the counter-examples help clarify the concept being described? In this instance, you could use five good examples of how to write a particular question, and not clarify the concept as much as you would by matching one good example with a single counter-example.

Another really useful way to use counter-examples is to use them to present the information in the first place, rather than starting with the concepts.

For example, if you wanted to teach learners how to write a good job description, you could give them a few terrible job descriptions and then have them identify all the issues. Then you could use that learner-generated list to create the "good" guidelines.

HOW MUCH GUIDANCE?

I'm always anxious when I give people directions. I worry that I won't be clear enough and that people will wind up hopelessly lost, wandering in circles and cursing my very bad-directions-giving existence.

Creating a learning experience involves giving directions—ideally, ones that won't leave your learner wandering aimlessly.

So how do you prefer to give directions?

I give step-by-step instructions–the person just needs to follow them exactly, and they'll be fine.

I like to sketch out a map that shows all the big streets, and then draw their specific route to it.

I don't really like to give directions unless I can put the actual map in front of a person so they can see the bigger picture.

You know what's really an underappreciated skill? Compass reading. More people should know how to navigate with a compass.

On one end of the spectrum, we have all the details spelled out exactly, and at the other end of the spectrum, we have an approach that is all conceptual.

HOW DO YOU GIVE DIRECTIONS?

If mapping out someone's learning experience requires you to give directions, what's the best tactic for helping your learners get to their destinations?

STEP-BY-STEP DIRECTIONS

If you need to get your learners somewhere, you can just give them precise step-by-step directions throughout.

I give step-by-step instructions–the person just needs to follow them exactly, and they'll be fine.

Pro: The learners are likely to be able to do the task pretty quickly by following the instructions.

Con: If something happens that falls outside the directions, then the learner will be pretty much stuck.

Let's say you are giving someone driving directions—someone completely unfamiliar with the area where you live. You tell that person "Turn at the hair salon with the big purple sign," but the hair salon got taken over last week by a tattoo parlor that painted over the sign with a skull motif. Now your person is basically lost, and they don't have any way to self-correct because they don't have any concept of the big picture or any general sense of the neighborhood that will allow them to troubleshoot.

If it's too easy to follow the individual directions, then the learner won't learn.

When I'm driving in an unfamiliar city, I love my GPS device—it's much simpler than dealing with maps and directions, but it's not a good way to learn my way around a city. If I'm trying to get familiar with a new place, working from a map is much better. This goes back to the friction idea. A little extra effort can be useful for remembering.

The GPS is the low-friction choice. If you just want people to get there, exact instructions or a GPS are great (and that may be the best choice sometimes), but if you want people to learn how to get there, you want the process to be more effortful on the part of the learner.

DIY NAVIGATION — LEARNING ALL THE CONCEPTS AND PRINCIPLES

You can teach them all the concepts and principles they would need operate and troubleshoot.

Pro: They'll really know how. You can drop them in the middle of the Sonoran Desert and, given the basic tools, they'll be able to find their way out.

Con: It's overkill.

Unless you need people to understand at that level, you can choose a faster, more expedient method. It takes a long time to get people to understand the conceptual material at that level, and if you need to make them experts before they can do much with it, then it's probably not the most practical solution.

WAYFINDING — THE MIDDLE GROUND

Overall, it looks like the cons outweigh the pros in those two extremes. The answer is probably in the middle, between exact instructions and high-level concepts, because, remember, you don't only want your learners to be able to get where they're going, but you want other things for them as well:

- They should be able take what they've learned and apply it in multiple circumstances.

- They should be able to troubleshoot when things don't go quite as expected.
- They should have confidence about their ability to get where they are going.

APPLYING THE LEARNING IN MULTIPLE CIRCUMSTANCES

One of the biggest challenges when teaching skills is getting those skills to transfer to the real world, in multiple contexts.

Here's an example. A while ago I did a nifty little tutorial on how to make an envelope icon in PowerPoint (from the wonderful *Rapid E-Learning Blog* by Tom Kuhlmann, www.articulate.com/rapid-elearning).

This is what I created:

OK, it's not going to win any design awards, but for me it was a banner effort. And it made me wonder, based on this learning experience, how many other well-designed icons am I able to create?

Well, pretty much none. Zero, zip, zilch.

I created this with the tutorial equivalent of a GPS giving me turn-by-turn instructions. Left to my own devices, I simply don't know enough to apply this to other types of things. For example, I tried to make a coffee cup icon on my own, and this is what I came up with:

Not great. It pretty much looks like a roll of toilet paper with a handle.

So where did I go wrong? The problem wasn't with the tutorial, which did what it purported to do in easy, clear steps. If all I needed were to make envelope icons, it would be more than sufficient.

There are some concepts and skills that I need before I will be able to create decent-looking icons without the aid of step-by-step instructions. For example, I probably need to know things like:

- How to determine the light source
- Where to add shadows and highlights
- How to layer gradients and transparencies
- How to make an interesting composition

Given that I don't know what I don't know, I'm probably missing some things on that list.

Working though a single example is not sufficient to teach me the necessary concepts. So what's the best way to accomplish that?

OPTION 1: LOTS OF EXAMPLES

I could work through lots and lots of examples. Eventually, I would start to recognize patterns and start to automatically do certain things that I'd repeated over and over.

This isn't the worst method, but it's probably a bit on the slow side, and it assumes that someone has created all the tutorials with step-by-step directions for a dozen or more other icons.

Using lots of examples may be necessary when it's hard to be exact about the concepts being taught.

For example, if you were teaching salespeople to build rapport with their customers, how easy would it be to define exactly how to do that?

Probably not that easy, right? There are a few things you could say, like "be friendly" or "ask questions," but learners will have to use their judgment about what kind of questions, how many questions, when to stop asking questions before it becomes annoying, and so on.

Good rapport building is something we learn *tacitly*. We learn it by observing ourselves and others and by trying different things to see what works.

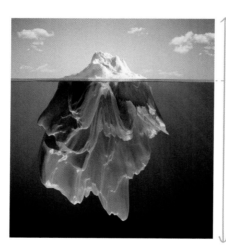

Explicit Rules
*Visible; can be
explained precisely*

Tacit Rules
*Not visible; hard to explain
precisely; often require
experience, practice, and
pattern recognition*

Explicit rules can be taught, but tacit rules can usually only be learned by seeing lots of examples and starting to recognize patterns. It's probably going to be necessary for the salespeople to see other examples of rapport building, or to experiment themselves, to learn the subtleties of it.

Because there are several explicit rules around drawing a coffee cup, it's probably not necessary or efficient to use just looking at examples as a teaching method. There are faster ways to go.

OPTION 2: CONCEPTS FOLLOWED BY EXAMPLES

The traditional method is to teach the concepts and then work on examples.

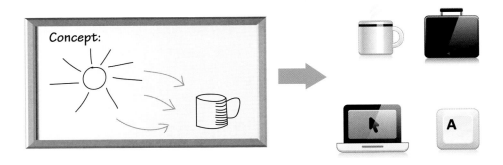

This is a reasonable approach, although you are asking your learners to understand the concepts without much up-front context.

OPTION 3: EXAMPLES FOLLOWED BY CONCEPTS

Let's say you have to drive to a destination that you've only been to once before. Are you more likely to remember how to get there if, on your previous visit, you:

a. Drove yourself, or
b. Were a passenger in the car?

There's a lot of benefit to letting learners drive themselves whenever possible.

One way to do so is to provide some examples, then let the learners help identify the concepts, rather than just telling them the concepts up front. After they've identified those concepts, they can apply them to additional examples. It could go something like this:

1. Work through some examples.
2. Have the students identify the concepts they saw in the examples.
3. Clarify the concepts and correct any misconceptions using the original examples as context.
4. Have the learners apply those concepts to further examples.

TROUBLESHOOTING

We've already talked about how another problem with step-by-step directions is that if learners step off the path for any reason, they are pretty much, well, lost in the woods.

Unless they have prior knowledge to tap into, they don't really have any way to troubleshoot issues that don't run true to the given path.

One way to address that is to make sure that the learner has a higher-level sense of what's going on:

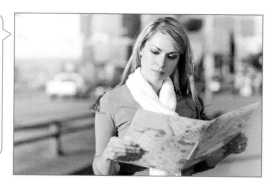

Although making sure the learner knows about the big picture can be helpful, the other way to prepare learner to troubleshoot variations is somewhat counterintuitive.

TELL THEM LESS, NOT MORE

Basically, if you want learners to be able to problem-solve and deal with variation, they need to practice doing just that. But as we looked at in Chapter 5, examples that lay everything out in a logical order don't really require the learners to practice those skills.

You can give them that practice opportunity by leaving some holes in your examples that they need to figure out how to fill in, or by letting them know where they need to get to but not all the details about how to get there.

Hmm, that stream wasn't on the map. I will have to figure out a way around it, if I want to keep my feet dry!

This is a little like having directions like "season to taste" in recipes. By having some gaps, rather than having only tidy, correct answers, learners are forced to figure out parts of the process themselves.

MAKE SURE THEY HAVE CONFIDENCE IN THEIR ABILITY

The best thing I got out of the envelope-icon tutorial (aside from a nifty envelope icon!) is the sense that I can, in the right circumstances, create something that doesn't look too bad.

While I was conscious at the time that those circumstances didn't add up to my being able to create those things without guidance, just the fact that I did it once meant that *it was possible*.

Look! I made that!

Ways for learners to gain confidence:

- **Have them do actual tasks, not just "activities based on the content."** If learners see some demonstrable evidence that they can actually *do* something with what they are learning, they'll be more likely to feel that way when they are trying to apply the knowledge later.
- **Make sure they have some early successes.** It's tempting to want to show them all the tricky, weird exceptions right off the bat, but it's good to start with tasks that will give learners early wins.
- **Let them work on their own problems.** Make sure that learners have the opportunity to take what they are learning and apply it to real challenges in their own work or lives.
- **Let them drive themselves.** We talked about it above, but it bears repeating: Wherever possible, let learners drive themselves, rather than having them be passengers in your car.

In the book *What the Best College Teachers Do*, professor Donald Saari talks about using a combination of stories and questions to challenge students to think critically about calculus:

> *"When I finish the process...I want the students to feel like they have invented calculus and that only some accident of birth kept them from beating Newton to the punch."*

A PROCESS TO FOLLOW

A model I really like, and frequently use in my own design work, is Michael Allen's CCAF model:

Context: *The framework and conditions*

Challenge: *A stimulus to action within the context*

Activity: *A physical response to the challenge*

Feedback: *A reflection of the effectiveness of the learner's action*

—*From* Michael Allen's Guide to e-Learning

Let's take a look at each of these steps in more detail, and at how each step would play out in a learning design.

SCENARIO: SUPERTECH

You've been asked to create a training program for the SuperTech customer service call center. SuperTech's latest smartphone product has some interesting... er...features, and the customer service people have been getting hammered with irate customer calls.

In this case, the learners—those put-upon customer service reps (CSRs)—are supposed to use a three-step process (validate, diffuse, and assist) when dealing with an irate customer.

STEP 1: DETERMINE CONTEXT

When I'm determining the context, I usually ask four questions:

- What is the general context for the task? For example, where does it come in the workflow, what is the purpose, and how often is it used?
- What is the emotional context for the task? For example, is the learner going to be under pressure or stress when they are using the knowledge? Are they going to be bored, or disrupted?
- What are the triggers that alert the learner that they will need to retrieve and use this knowledge? What's happening in their environment to let them know they need to do something?
- What is the physical context? Where are they, what objects are around them, and what or who are they interacting with?

If you got these answers to the questions, how would that impact your design for SuperTech?

- **General Context.** The CSRs get a variety of calls during the day. Most of these are run-of-the-mill calls. Irate calls have been increasing lately, but a CSR will still handle only one to three irate calls per shift and, depending on the shift, may have days without any irate calls.

  This helps you determine the interval. The CSRs may get two irate callers in a row, or may have an entire shift without any. Spreading out exposures to the material over time helps improve retention, which tells us we may want to have the training in chunks, spread out over a few days (we'll talk more about this in the next chapter).

- **Emotional Context.** CSRs operate in a high-pressure environment. They are expected to meet calls-per-hour quotas, and they have to be knowledgeable about a wide variety of products. In the past, CSRs had the option of passing off highly irate customers to a supervisor, although they were encouraged to handle calls themselves if they could. With the increase in "hot" customer calls due to problems with SuperTech's new smartphone product, CSRs are increasingly required to handle the calls, and they can pass them to supervisors only if the caller demands a supervisor or becomes verbally abusive. CSRs are being pushed out of their comfort zone and are feeling the stress of the unhappy customers, while continuing to have to meet their calls-per-hour goals despite the new situation.

We want the learners to become comfortable dealing with irate customers in a time-constrained environment while keeping calm themselves. Ideally, the training would mimic both the heightened emotional conditions and the time constraints. Learners could start with calmer, less time-constrained scenarios and then progress to more fraught, timed practice scenarios.

- **Triggers.** The customer's tone and wording are the cues that let the CSR know they are dealing with an irate caller.

  Part of the training should ensure that learners can recognize the signs or triggers that tell them they need to start using the validate–diffuse–assist process.

  In addition to practicing the "active" answers to the questions "is this an irate caller?" and "should I use the validate–diffuse–assist process with this caller?" the learner also needs to decide when they need to pass the caller on to a supervisor. These decision points should be built into the challenge and activity.

- **Physical Context.** The CSR clicks a button on their computer screen to indicate they are available for a new call, which they receive over their telephone headset. They frequently get the customer's record on their computer screen, but sometimes have to search for the customer record. They have access to a screen that shows what product the customer has purchased, the history of their service plan, and the CSR notes from any previous customer calls.

  This tells you which artifacts—the customer records screens and telephone headsets—should be used as part of the training if possible. The physical context helps create cognitive associations that will help the learner retrieve the information as needed.

STEP 2: CHALLENGE

The question to ask yourself here is, What is an appropriate real-world challenge or accomplishment that the learner would do?

In our SuperTech case, a possible challenge could be satisfying or appropriately handling a certain number of customers.

STEP 3: WHAT'S THE ACTIVITY?

There are a number of ways to handle the activity portion of your learning design. Think about how you would set the activity for the learner to perform before you read the suggestions below.

—TAKE A MOMENT TO CONSIDER WHAT YOU WOULD DO BEFORE MOVING ON—

DESIGN SUGGESTION: USE A PRE-ACTIVITY

Learners can be more prepared to learn if they have been primed ahead of time. Send out an email to ask the learners to collect a few irate customer problems and a few possible solutions they've already been using. Use these for scenarios or examples in the training (they can be sent to you as the learning designer or gathered in a central location such as an intranet).

DESIGN SUGGESTION: CREATE ELEARNING SCENARIOS

Depending on the size and geographic distribution of the audience, elearning may be a practical solution. Create scenarios in which learners need to use the validate–diffuse–assist process to lower the customer's heat level and successfully resolve the call.

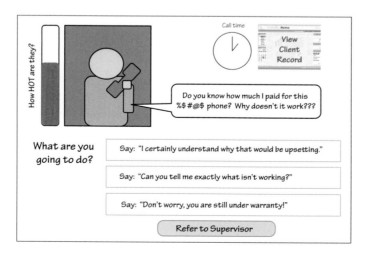

This design would need to have multiple scenarios, including a few that could be successfully resolved only by referring to the supervisor, and possibly one or two that didn't require the validate–diffuse–assist process because the customers weren't actually irate.

An effective way to get the learner started would be to have the first scenario be a walkthrough. Have you ever played a video game where the first level is heavily guided to introduce you to the game? A similar technique can be useful in elearning. A first, untimed scenario could be a way to get familiar with the interface and with the validate–diffuse–assist process.

Ideally, the learners wouldn't do all the scenarios in one sitting. Instead, they would be spread out over a few days. For example, you could have the learner tackle three scenarios a day for three days. This way, the learner would have multiple exposures to the material, and the distribution would be closer to the distribution they would have in real life. Additionally, learners would have to refresh themselves on the validate–diffuse–assist process over multiple days, which would help consolidate their memory.

Keep in mind that this is only a *recognition* activity—unfacilitated elearning is not a good medium for providing successful *recall* activities, because while computers can give quite good feedback on options that a learner selects, they aren't so adept at handling things the learner *recalls* (e.g., says or writes). So elearning may be a reasonable way to learn about the validate–diffuse–assist process, but not as good a way to practice or develop the skills of using it.

Ugly Prototypes!

If the image on the previous page looks rough, and like something drawn quickly in PowerPoint, that's probably because it was. This is actually the kind of quick and dirty prototype that I would create for a client. A detailed look at production process for elearning is beyond the scope of this book, but I strongly advocate for rapid prototyping as a way of sketching out designs. I typically don't spend a lot of time storyboarding the design before prototyping. As soon as we have the goals and audience and context defined, I start creating actual layouts and prototypes. There are different tools that can be used to prototype, but even PowerPoint can be used to create semi-functional prototypes by hyperlinking in the document.

DESIGN SUGGESTION: USE ROLE-PLAYS

It's going to be extremely difficult to try to simulate the emotional context of dealing with an irate customer without person-to-person role-plays. Because all the real-life interactions take place over the phone, the role-plays could take place in a classroom setting or even over the phone.

Role-plays can be done with the instructor or with other students. An instructor may be better at simulating an angry client, but using student-to-student role-plays can be a really practical way to give learners more practice opportunities.

As a starting point, you can give people a quick character sketch and talking points, and you can model a few role-plays in front of the whole group before having students work with each other. You also want to model critiquing the role-play, and give the students a structured feedback form, so they can evaluate together how well the process was followed.

DESIGN SUGGESTION: BLENDED LEARNING

If the scope of the project supports it, a combination of all the above strategies can be an effective way to address this problem from multiple perspectives and to make the most of the role-play activities by getting familiarization with validate–diffuse–assist out of the way using the elearning scenarios to introduce the process. That way, learners can spend class time actively practicing rather than listening to a description of the process.

DESIGN SUGGESTION: FOLLOW-UP ACTIVITIES AND JOB AIDS

The best way to support the continuation of a learned behavior is to give it some ongoing support. For example, you could distribute a take-away job aid that listed strategies for the validate–diffuse–assist process. Even better, give them a template, and have them create their own job aid so it will be more meaningful to them.

Additionally, follow-up elearning scenarios could get sent out over the few weeks after the training, at the rate of one customer per week, to refresh learners on the process. There could be an intranet site with a discussion forum that allowed learners to document effective strategies and answers they used with irate clients. The best suggestions could be circulated via email to the whole audience. Any of these ideas would keep refreshing the process for the learners.

STEP 4: HOW ARE YOU GIVING THE LEARNER FEEDBACK?

Let's take a closer look at the details of some feedback options, bearing in mind that some feedback options are somewhat determined by the nature of the activity.

FEEDBACK IN THE ELEARNING SCENARIO

There are a variety of ways the elearning scenario can give feedback. There can be the client reaction, which can be not only what the client says but also the client's facial expression and the client's tone of voice (if audio is used). There can also be a "heat" meter that shows whether the client is getting calmer or hotter. These are all good ways to "show" rather than "tell." There can be more traditional "tell" feedback ("Good choice!") if absolutely necessary, but we want to leverage "showing" as much as possible. Ultimately the main source of feedback is the outcome—is the learner successful with the client? If not, they should probably have to try again until they are successful.

FEEDBACK IN THE ROLE-PLAYS

Feedback in face-to-face role-plays isn't as clear-cut as in an elearning environment, because the learner isn't selecting from options and could say anything. However, there are some ways to structure the feedback to make it more effective:

- Have a feedback sheet that the "customer" or an observer could fill out, tracking how well the learner followed the process. The sheet could have a combination of checkboxes and short answer spaces so as to be quick to fill out but also flexible.
- Use a similar feedback sheet to allow learners to assess their own performance in the role-plays.
- The "customer" could have a set of "heat cards" that represented how irate they were supposed to be. As the learner effectively calms the customer, the customer could hand over heat cards, or could take them back if their "anger" level goes back up. If the learner can successfully get at least 80 percent of the cards, they would get credit for that customer.

ONGOING COACHING FEEDBACK

Ultimately, the best feedback would be ongoing coaching based on real performance. To do this, a supervisor could periodically listen in (a common practice in call centers) and provide detailed and specific feedback to the learner.

SUMMARY

- Use strategies such as recall of prior knowledge and metacognition to help support memory encoding and retrieval.
- Some friction is necessary in learning. Just telling them is too smooth, and it won't stick. Learners frequently need to engage with the material to retain it.
- Social interaction can be an effective way to add friction to learning.
- Whenever possible, show, don't tell.
- The right content is less than you think it is, has enough detail but no more, and is relevant to the learners.
- Starting with or using counter-examples can be a good way to prevent misconceptions.
- Decide how much guidance you need to give your learners. Resist the urge to hold their hand at every moment.
- A successful learning experience should leave the learner feeling confident and successful—"like they invented calculus."
- You can use CCAF (Context, Challenge, Activity, and Feedback) to design effective learning experiences.

REFERENCES

Bain, Ken. 2004. *What the Best College Teachers Do*. Cambridge: Harvard University Press.

Barrows, Howard S. 1996. "Problem-Based Learning in Medicine and Beyond: A Brief Overview." *New Directions for Teaching and Learning: Bringing Problem-Based Learning to Higher Education: Theory and Practice, No. 68*. Wilkerson, Luann and Wim Gijselaers (Eds). San Francisco: Jossey-Bass.

Heath, Chip and Dan Heath. 2007. *Made to Stick: Why Some Ideas Survive and Others Die*. New York: Random House.

Kuperberg, Gina R., Balaji M. Lakshmanan, David N. Caplan, and Philip J. Holcomb. 2006. "Making Sense of Discourse: An fMRI Study of Causal Inferencing Across Sentences." *NeuroImage* 33: 343–361.

Moore, Cathy. 2011. Checklist for Strong Learning Design. *Cathy Moore: Let's Save the World from Boring Training*. http://blog.cathy-moore.com/2011/07/checklist-for-strong-elearning.

Muller, D. A. 2008. "Designing Effective Multimedia for Physics Education." PhD thesis (School of Physics, University of Sydney).

Rich, Lani Diane and Alastair Stephens. 2011. "Show and Tell." *StoryWonk Daily*. http://storywonk.com/storywonk-daily-102-show-and-tell/.

Sweller, John. 1988. "Cognitive Load During Problem Solving: Effects on Learning." *Cognitive Science* (June). 12 (2): 257–285.

DESIGN FOR SKILLS

(IN WHICH WE LEARN THAT NOBODY WANTS TO BIKE STRAIGHT UPHILL
ALL THE TIME AND THAT IF YOU DON'T GIVE YOUR LEARNERS
CHANCES TO REST, THEY'LL TAKE THEM ANYWAY)

DEVELOPING SKILLS

Teaching skills is not for the easily daunted. It takes time and effort and practice, both for you and for your learner.

In Chapter 1 we looked at the question you can use to determine if something is a skill:

> *Is it reasonable to think that someone can be proficient without practice?*

If the answer is "no, it's not reasonable," then you know you are dealing with a skill.

Here's the thing. A lot of learning experiences purport to teach a skill, when really all they do is *introduce* the skill.

There's nothing wrong with just introducing a learner to a skill. An introduction familiarizes the learner with the skills, and that's a necessary first step. If you've been given the task of creating a one-hour introduction to windsurfing or tamale making or spreadsheet editing, then you are just introducing learners to that skill, and that's the scope of the learning experience.

But if you are actually trying to get your learners to some level of proficiency with a skill, then there's a little bit more involved.

There are two main components to developing a skill: **practice** and **feedback**.

PRACTICE

We've already addressed the fact that just handing a learner information doesn't make them proficient. A salesperson could have all the features of a product memorized, but that's only a tiny part of what makes them competent or skilled at their job.

Learners need to practice with the relevant skills and information before they can develop proficiency, but all too often they just get a single dose of training on a topic or skill. For example, a salesperson might attend a two-hour lecture on product features, with the expectation that that will be enough for sales-people to sell that product proficiently.

The truth is that anything that is "learned" through lecture must be put into long-term memory through practice. It gets practiced on the job.

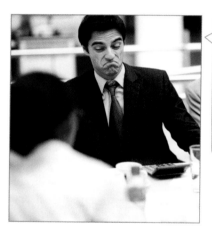

Either you give your learners the opportunity to practice, or they'll practice on their own. It might be a more painful process, and it might not be the kind of practice you want them to have...

There's a bunch of extra steps that we're supposed to go through here to determine which product model, but, ya know? I find that the mid-size really works for just about everybody, and it really saves on paperwork...

In other words, you either create opportunities for learners to practice, or you take what you get. But first, let's look (again) at the brain.

What's going on in your brain when you are learning something new? You're putting forth a lot of effort, and subsequently using a lot of glucose (the simple sugar that is one of the primary sources of energy in the body).

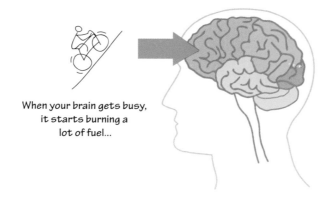

When your brain gets busy, it starts burning a lot of fuel...

Basically, learning a lot of new information is the cognitive equivalent of biking uphill.

You make heavy use of such areas of the brain as your frontal cortex (the rational, reasoning, concentration-y part of the brain). You can overload it pretty easily. Ever had the experience of taking in so much new information that your head kind of hurts?

How about when you are using something you already know? When you are using learned behaviors, your brain runs much more efficiently and uses less glucose.

Familiar skills don't require nearly as much conscious attention.

When you're performing a familiar, learned behavior, it's more like the cognitive equivalent of coasting downhill.

This image (Haier 1992) show how much glucose a brain burns when learning how to play the video game Tetris (on the left) compared to the same brain after several weeks of practice (on the right). Even when playing a much harder level of Tetris, the practiced brain is likely to require significantly less energy.

STRUCTURING PRACTICE

The goal of practice is eventually to get to proficiency and unconscious competence. Depending on the scope of your learning experience, that may or may not be a realistic goal, but we do want to move people along the path toward that.

THE STRUCTURE PROBLEM: TOO MUCH OF THE NEW

Most learning experiences are structured around lots of new information. Lots and *lots* of new information:

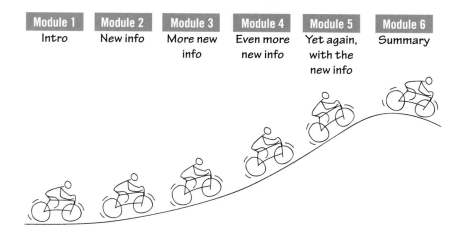

The problem with this is that it's exhausting for your learners. Do you really want to ask a new learner to bike straight uphill for the entire lesson? (Note: bicycling images are based on work I did at Allen Interactions and are used with their generous permission.)

How else could learning experiences be structured? An alternative structure for learning would be to switch between these approaches, to allow the learner to acclimate and assimilate the information before moving to the next level (incidentally, this is how many games are structured).

Level 1	Level 2	Level 3	Level 4	Level 5	Level 6
Some new stuff, pretty easy, though	Stuff you know plus a bit more	Stuff you know, maybe a little faster	Stuff you know plus a bit more	Stuff you know, kicked up a notch	Boss Fight!

If the learner can't get up a part of the hill, they get to try again until they succeed. This ensures that the learner won't get into difficult territory until they are ready, and that they are staying at the edge of their ability level.

EFFECTIVE PRACTICE IS A LOT LIKE FLOW

Have you ever been so engaged in an activity that you looked up and realized hours had passed, but it felt like only 15 minutes had gone by because you were so intensely engaged in what you were doing?

If so, you might have been experiencing what the Czech psychologist Mihaly Csikszentmihalyi called *flow*, which he describes as "joy, creativity, the process of total involvement with life."

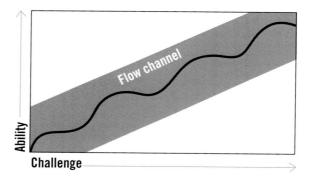

While Csikszentmihalyi's flow model has several aspects to it, one of the core tenets is a balance between ability and challenge.

When the challenge far exceeds a learner's ability, it's probably too difficult for that learner and it quickly becomes frustrating. But when something is far too easy for a learner, it's boring. On the other hand, something that is *slightly* too hard can be a satisfying challenge, and something that is a little bit easy can be a satisfying opportunity to coast for a few minutes.

Keeping people on *that edge between challenge and ability* is one of the fundamental principles of flow. Ideally, learning practice would allow learners a balance of challenge and satisfaction.

PAYING ATTENTION TO WHAT'S DIFFERENT

Another benefit of giving learners the opportunity to coast occasionally is that it allows them to pay attention to what's different.

When it's all new information, it's all uphill:

In the straight-uphill model, everything is new and everything is important, so therefore nothing is.

But when you balance the experience, the new material stands out:

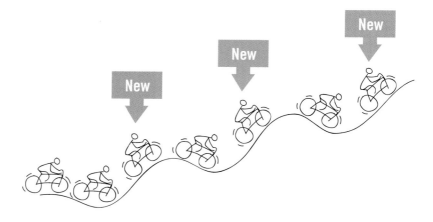

Not only does it stand out, but your learner has the energy to absorb it and hasn't habituated to the influx of information.

And remember, if you don't give your learners breaks, they'll take them anyway:

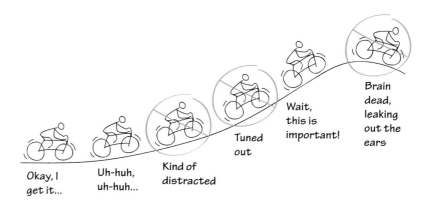

WHAT DOES STRUCTURING PRACTICE LOOK LIKE?

So how could this play out in practical terms? I once worked with a client that had a large team of sales/service people. Their job had a steep learning curve, because there were technical aspects of how to fix machines with a very wide range of complicated products. The client considered the employees to be salespeople first and service people second, so they were very interested in improving sales skills. Also, the sales/service people were expected to run their territories like their own business and to have the skills and knowledge to do that.

The client wanted to add elearning to their curriculum, because the then-current training for new hires consisted of a two-week class in which they basically tried to give the learners as much information as they could possibly absorb, followed by some job-shadowing and some feedback ride-alongs with their managers.

So it's no wonder the client wanted to add elearning to their curriculum. What they were doing was basically like biking straight uphill for two weeks without a break. Learners were effectively being asked to jam five years' worth of new clothes into a space the size of a gym locker. As you can imagine, they had a tough time taking everything in, and an even tougher time retaining it. As a result, many learned on the job in hit-or-miss fashion. It's a testament to the strong culture of the organization that the ones who survived often did quite well, but the client felt they could do better and wanted a curriculum that did a better job of developing skills over time.

The revised curriculum looked like this:

- An initial in-person class shortened to a few days
- Job-shadowing with an experienced employee
- The remainder of the curriculum spread out over two dozen simulated sales calls intended to be completed within two to three months
- Follow-up assignments to be performed in the field based on the content learned in each elearning module
- A field assessment system that had checklists of all the crucial competencies (technical, product, sales, etc.), with which managers verified that the learners could actually do all the necessary tasks
- Follow-up or reinforcement classes as needed

This program didn't require the learner to grasp all the information all at once. Instead it was spread out over time. By the time the learner finished the last few elearning models, they already had a few months of experience to provide context.

Then, managers, using the field assessment system, could figure out pretty quickly where there were gaps, and use review of the relevant elearning lesson and face-to-face coaching to try to address those gaps. The revised program was able to provide feedback loops to help verify and improve competencies.

SPACING OUT THE PRACTICE OVER TIME

How many times does someone need to practice something, and how often?

SCENARIO: RECYCLING

You are a recycling coordinator for your medium-sized town, and part of your job is to educate the public about how to sort their recycling.

Most of the folks are pretty environmentally oriented, so you don't have much trouble getting people to go through your recycling training classes, but you are noticing that people just aren't following through.

They do a good job the first time they recycle after the class, but after that they pretty quickly forget the right things to do. Part of the problem is that recycling for common materials (paper, cans, and glass) happens only every two weeks, and recycling for less common items (some plastics, batteries, etc.) happens only once a month. Most of your issues are with the less common items.

How would you space the practice to support learning?

— TAKE A MOMENT TO CONSIDER WHAT YOU WOULD DO BEFORE MOVING ON —

You consider a few options for how to correct this problem:

- You could add an extra 30 minutes to the class so that people could get extra hands-on recycling practice and *really* learn the behavior.
- You could do a follow-up email every day for two weeks, with an online link to a recycling practice game in which people could practice what they learned.
- You could send the online link for the recycling practice game once a month for the next year.

If you could choose only one option for maximum long-term retention, which option do you think would work the best? ▧

This is actually a pretty well-researched question. Basically, is practice better if it's all massed together or if it's distributed over time?

The answer depends somewhat on what's being studied, but for the most part **you want to distribute your learning over time if possible**.

The first time you learn something, you obviously want to spend enough time to ensure you have a good grasp on the material, but extra practice **at that time** will provide a diminishing return.

HOW LONG SHOULD YOU WAIT?

Somewhat counterintuitively, a longer period in between practice sessions can lead to longer overall retention. A good rule of thumb is to time the practices to how often you'll need to use the behavior.

Say you are teaching your aunt Joan how to attach pictures to her emails and you want her to *really* learn it so that she stops making you come over once or twice a week to do it for her. How often would you want Aunt Joan to practice?

You would probably have her practice the task one or two times a week until she is able to competently do it herself, to match how frequently she is going to retrieve and use the knowledge later.

If that's not practical (Uncle Carlos has the same problem but is only going to be in town for a week), then you want, at a minimum, to at least spread the practice over several days. There seems to be a benefit in sleeping between learning reinforcements. The act of sleeping seems to help consolidate what people learn, so having practice over multiple days takes advantage of that phenomenon.

The best choice for the recycling training would be a reminder once a month, since it was the monthly recycling items that were posing the biggest problems for the learners. Additionally, if you could time the reminder to come a day or two before the particular learner's recycling date, the practice exercise would also act as a job or a reference that a person could consult if unsure.

HOW MUCH PRACTICE?

A few variables influence the amount of practice that you need:

- **How variable the outcomes are**—there are probably only a few right ways to check a patient's blood pressure, but there might be hundreds of right ways to design a website. If correct performance is highly variable (like the website example) then learners will probably need more practice scenarios than something with low variability (the blood pressure example).
- **How low does the error rate need to be**—if you are creating training for flight attendants it's likely the safety procedures need to have a lower error rate than the procedures for drink service. Low error or error-free performance will require more practice than more error-tolerant topics.
- **What level of automaticity is required**—if you need to get someone to the point where they are performing with a high degree of automaticity, or unconscious competence, then a high degree of practice is required.
- **How quickly do they need to respond**—if people need to react very quickly to an infrequent situation, then lots of practice, role-plays, and spaced reinforcement should be part of your learning design. If people will have enough time to access a job aid, then it's more important to ensure that they know when and where to access that resource.

FEEDBACK

In order for practice to be effective, learners need to be able to tell how they are doing. This is particularly important for skill development, because practicing something incorrectly can be worse than not practicing at all. The incorrect skill can become ingrained, and then correcting that skill later will require unlearning behaviors that have become automatic.

We looked at some of the characteristics of good feedback in the previous chapter (e.g., show don't tell; consequence-based feedback), but there are a few other considerations that you may want to think about when providing feedback for practice and skill development.

FREQUENCY OF FEEDBACK

If you've ever played video games, you were probably thinking "Wow! Look at the corrective feedback mechanisms for shaping behavior that are in this game!"

OK, you probably *weren't* thinking that, but if you were, award yourself a learning-nerd power-up.

I bring up games again because they are fantastic little laboratories of skill development, and a big part of why games are so good at developing skills is the frequency and variety of feedback mechanisms. Most modern video games give the player feedback every few seconds. Even a slower game will give feed-back every few minutes.

So how often do (non–video-game) learners typically get feedback? A worst-case scenario might be the college lecture class that has two grades—the midterm and the final. A student could be veering off course for *months* before getting any course correction.

The good news is that if you use the Context, Challenge, Activity, and Feedback model, or if you design a curriculum around structured goals, you have lots of built-in feedback points. You should look for opportunities to increase the frequency of feedback whenever possible.

VARIETY OF FEEDBACK

Let's say that video game you play has the immediate goal of killing as many zombies as possible. And let's say that every time you killed a zombie, a pop-up box appeared that said "Good Job. You successfully killed a zombie! Click the Continue button to continue!"

I'd call that a candidate for Worst Game Ever at that point.

Increasing the frequency of feedback is great, but if you do that, you also want to have *various ways* to provide feedback.

If we look at games again, we see that video games use feedback devices like sounds, points, character reactions, scores, and visual cues. Live games such as board games or kids' games also have feedback mechanisms that don't involve slamming the action to a halt and explicating or stating something. In Monopoly, you don't get lectured about poor business choices—you lose money or go bankrupt or go to jail.

FOLLOW-UP COACHING

The feedback that happens after the learning experience is over should be like good coaching. It helps the learner understand where they are doing things right, where they are doing things wrong, and what they should try instead.

Frequency matters here as well. The typical workplace format is to give performance reviews on an annual basis. How useful do you think that is for shaping behaviors?

Yeah, frequently not at all. Providing coaching and feedback only on an annual basis is like predicting the weather: The farther out it goes, the more inaccurate it gets.

Figuring out when the check-ins need to occur can be enormously helpful. Part of designing your learning experience should be setting a schedule.

- When are you going to follow up?
- What will be evaluated?
- What criteria will be used?

This gives learners an opportunity to head for the goal.

Specific Criteria Make your feedback extra-helpful by using explicit, standard-ized criteria. A feedback sheet or checklist can also make it feasible for the learner to self-assess, which can be useful both for practical considerations and in keeping the learner aware of the criteria.

OTHER WAYS TO FOLLOW UP

If the structure and setup of your learning situation don't allow for coaching follow-up, there are other ways to reach out and follow up with learners:

- Create a forum online and encourage learners to report back on their experiences.
- Send periodic emails with examples, tips, and opportunities for learners to self-evaluate.
- Have virtual critique sessions that allow learners to post work and get feedback from the community.

DESIGN FOR ACCOMPLISHMENTS

Once your learners have mastered skills, they should be able to go into the world and accomplish tasks requiring those skills. For example, an art student learns graphic design skills, so she can successfully accomplish tasks like designing a brochure, laying out a website, or creating a logo. You can use accomplishments as a way to structure your learning design. Let's take a look at an example. Remember Todd, our new restaurant manager from Chapter 3? You are creating a new version of a course to train Todd and other new restaurant managers. Your target audience is folks who have a fair amount of restaurant experience in other capacities (servers, kitchen staff, etc.) and who are moving into man-agement roles.

The course is supposed to cover everything from the basic elements (e.g., how to verify employee timesheets) all the way up to high-level strategy thinking about the restaurant as a business (e.g., the market position of the restaurant).

The old course is a series of modules:

- Hiring and managing staff
- Safety
- Ordering and inventory
- Bar and beverage sales
- Restaurant financials
- Customer service
- Health and quality control
- Marketing and promotion

The old course has pretty good content in it, but the students seem to be struggling on the job. Even if they did well in the course, they don't remember a lot of the information once they started work, and they have a hard time applying a lot of the information when they do remember it. Most eventually learn what they need to know, although a lot wash out along the way, which is a waste of time and money. Most of them also continue to struggle with taking the strategic view, even after they've figured out the day-to-day stuff.

We discussed the necessity for repetition and practice if you want to develop skills, but the current course structure doesn't allow for that. Once a learner finishes with the Safety module, they don't revisit it, even though the ability to spot safety violations as soon as they occur is an important skill for managers.

In restructuring the restaurant-manager course, you want the students to actually develop the necessary skills, and to be more ready to hit the ground running when they get on the job. You want the course to help develop skills, not just deliver information. How could you restructure the course to give the learners a chance to practice more, and to have multiple exposures to different items? Let's take a look at one possibility that uses a structure based on games.

HOW GAMES ARE STRUCTURED

We want to build skills and expertise, and we've already talked a little about how games are really good at this, but let's take a closer look at how games do this.

James Paul Gee, a scholar who studies video games for learning, describes it this way:

> Expertise is formed in any area by repeated cycles of learners practicing skills until they are nearly automatic, then having those skills fail in ways that cause the learners to have to think again and learn anew. Then they practice this new skill set to an automatic level of mastery only to see it, too, eventually be challenged.

> Good games create and support the cycle of expertise, with cycles of extended practice, tests of mastery of that practice, then a new challenge, and then new extended practice. This is, in fact, part of what constitutes good pacing in a game (Gee 2004).

One of the ways that games structure these cycles of expertise is by having immediate, short-term, medium-term, and long-term accomplishments for the learner.

So, for example, in the video game Diner Dash, you play the character of Flo, a waitress. Your immediate goals are to seat people, take orders, deliver food, and clear tables. Your short-term goal is to successfully complete a shift in the diner. Your medium-term goal is to upgrade to a better restaurant. Your long-term goal is to win the game. If you fail at lower goals, you can't move on to higher goals, and you have to practice until you are proficient enough to succeed.

Sebastian Deterding, a games researcher, uses this graphic to show a structured flow of goals (Deterding 2011):

The accomplishment of short-term goals is necessary to achieve the longer-term goals, which in turn roll up to accomplish the overarching goals.

If you were using this structure for a sales course, you might have this as your set of goals:

Time Frame	Goal
Immediate goal	Gather relevant data about different customers and their needs
Short-term goal	Determine a product and sales approach for different clients based on their needs
Medium-term goal	Succeed in closing with the client (make the sale, get the meeting, get the referral)
Long-term goal	Hit your sales quota for the quarter and win a trip to Hawaii

So instead of having a sales course that's structured with a module about determining customer needs, followed by a module on product features and benefits, followed by a module about the sales process with the client, you have a series of goals, and if you fail at any goal, you have to practice and try again until you succeed.

Another course I've seen this applied to taught police officers how to recognize possible warning signs for terrorism (Allen Interactions 2010):

Time Frame	Goal
Immediate goal	Gather relevant data at different incident sites
Short-term goal	Determine whether an individual incident needed to be reported, and if so, what data supported that conclusion
Medium-term goal	Successfully complete a day on patrol after investigating two to four incidents
Long-term goal	Head off the terrorist attack

There are a couple of big benefits to this way of structuring a learning experience:

- Learners are practicing the actual behaviors that they need to perform in the real world.
- Learners don't progress until they can master the necessary elements.
- Learners get multiple exposures to the concepts and material, and develop increased proficiency with those multiple exposures.
- Learners can have some success in the environment, because they can almost always achieve some of the goals, but they get specific feedback.
- Increasing levels of challenge, and new goals to pursue, keep the learner engaged.

HOW TO USE THIS FOR LEARNING

Let's say you've signed up to run a marathon, and when you check in to pick up your number, the organizer tells you that it's a free-form marathon, that you should just start running due west, and that after 26 miles you'll find the finish line.

"Exactly 26 miles, due west" is an exact destination, but it's not a very satisfying one, because you won't know if you are on course or not or how much progress you're making. Your learners want to know where they need to head to next, and they want feedback on how they are doing while getting there.

So let's go back to our restaurant management course.

How could you structure the course differently using short-term, medium-term, and long-term goals? Consider your answer before looking at one possible design solution outlined below.

Time Frame	Goal
Immediate goal	Respond to specific challenges that happen during a shift (late employee, unhappy customer, paperwork, cashing out, safety issues, etc.)
Short-term goal	Successfully complete a dinner shift
Medium-term goal	Successfully complete a full week, including financials, inventory, ordering, employee issues, and so on.
Long-term goal	Successfully complete a quarter, including hiring, menu planning, marketing, and strategic planning for the next quarter

In this scenario, the learner could focus on the immediate skills needed to survive a restaurant shift first, such as supervising employees, paperwork, dealing with an inventory shortage, and so on.

Then the learner could step back and focus on the skills for managing the restaurant for a week, such as scheduling, longer-term employee issues, inventory, and financials.

After that, the learner could focus on the skills necessary to manage the restaurant longer term—quarterly planning, hiring, teambuilding, marketing, menu planning, and ordering.

This way, instead of learning all about one topic in a single sitting and then moving on to the next topic, they would get multiple exposures to a topic over time. For example, you could address safety in a specific incident at the shift level, in preparing for an inspection at the week level, and in improving safety records at the quarterly level. That way, the topic of safety would be addressed multiple times over the entire course.

Always being able to see the next goal, and knowing what you need to work on next, is another characteristic of Csikszentmihalyi's flow model. This structure both spaces the learners' exposure to the content and ensures that there's always another goal to accomplish, thereby guiding them through the content.

SUMMARY

- Teaching skills requires two main elements: practice and feedback.
- Learners will practice with you or without you, but you may not like what they are practicing when they do it without you.
- Brain function gets more efficient with practice.
- Avoid a steady stream of new information—it's exhausting to your learners. Instead, build in opportunities for your learners to get a little proficiency with the new information before you move to the next element.
- If you don't give your learners a chance to rest, they'll take it anyway.
- Flow is a state of engagement that can be created through a balance of challenge and ability.
- Space practice out over time.
- You will need more practice if automatic or error-free performance is required.
- Promote engagement by using structured goals and real accomplishments.
- Use frequent and multifaceted feedback to shape behavior.
- When assessing learner performance, have them perform the actual task whenever possible.

REFERENCES

Allen Interactions. 2010. *Custom e-Learning: Allen Interactions—Law Enforcement Response to Terrorism.* www.youtube.com/watch?v=Vt8xkOTqwjg.

Csikszentmihalyi, Mihaly. 1990. *Flow: The Psychology of Optimal Experience.* New York: HarperCollins.

Deterding, Sebastian. 2011. Don't Play Games With Me! Presentation on slideshare.net; www.slideshare.net/dings/dont-play-games-with-me-promises-and-pitfalls-of-gameful-design?from=ss_embed, slide 63.

Gee, James Paul. 2004. "Learning by Design: Games as Learning Machines." *Gamasutra magazine.* www.gamasutra.com/gdc2004/features/20040324/gee_01.shtml.

Haier, R.J., B.V. Siegel Jr., A. MacLachlan, E. Soderling, S. Lottenberg, and M.S. Buchsbaum. 1992. "Regional Glucose Metabolic Changes after Learning a Complex Visuospatial/Motor Task: A Positron Emission Tomographic Study." *Brain Research* 570: 134-14.

Thalheimer, Will. 2006. "Spacing Learning Events Over Time." *Work-Learning Research, Inc.* www.work-learning.com/catalog.

DESIGN FOR
MOTIVATION

(IN WHICH WE LEARN THAT WE DON'T ALWAYS LEARN
THE RIGHT THING WHEN WE LEARN FROM EXPERIENCE,
AND THAT THE ELEPHANT IS A CREATURE OF HABIT)

We've already spent a lot of time looking at motivation to *learn* (remember the elephant?), so this chapter concerns itself with what motivates learners to *do*. Sometimes learners will have the knowledge and skills they need but still won't actually do the right things. You can't necessarily fix that as a learning designer, but there are things you can do to help.

MOTIVATION TO DO

Numerous studies have come out in the last few years that say texting while driving is a very, very dangerous thing to do.

Shocking.

That texting while driving is dangerous probably isn't a surprise to the vast majority of the population. So why do people continue to do it? I don't know exactly, but I suspect it's because people have one, or a mix, of the following thoughts and responses:

- *"I know it's a bad idea, and I never do it (except when I do, and then I feel guilty)."*
- *"I know it's a bad idea, but I only do it once in a while, and I'm very careful."*
- *"I know it's a bad idea for other people, but I can do it because I'm really good at it."*
- *"Huh? What's the big deal?"*

Most of the responses above indicate that this is not a knowledge problem, and that an intervention that focuses on knowledge isn't going to change anything, because it's not the "know" part but rather the "do" part of the sentence that's the problem.

So why do people *do* things they *know* are a bad idea? It's not because they aren't smart people. If it's not a knowledge problem, then more knowledge probably won't help.

A big part of this goes back to our elephant and rider. Frequently, the rider *knows*, but the elephant still *does*.

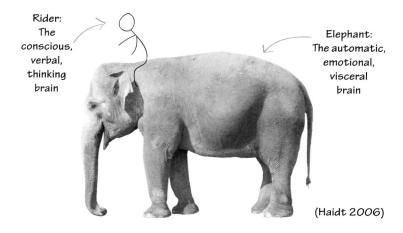

Rider: The conscious, verbal, thinking brain

Elephant: The automatic, emotional, visceral brain

(Haidt 2006)

WE LEARN FROM EXPERIENCE

Part of the reason for "I *know*, but..." is that people learn from *experience*, which is a great thing (we wouldn't want to live in a world where people didn't), but it can cause some problems. The elephant in particular can be far more influenced by experience than by abstract knowledge.

Here's an example. Let's say that 1 in 10 instances of texting while driving results in an accident (this isn't a real statistic; I don't think that exact data is known—this is just for purposes of argument). Let's take a look at the experience of two different drivers:

Perceived Usefulness	Perceived Ease of Use
Does the learner see this change as something that will be useful to them?	Does the learner see this change as something that will be easy to use or implement?

It's not a complicated idea—if you want someone to use something, they need to believe that it's actually useful and that it won't be a major pain in the butt to use.

TAM specifically addresses technology adoption, but those variables make sense in a lot of other areas as well.

I keep TAM in mind when I design anything that requires adopting a new technology, system, or practice (which is almost everything I do). Some of the questions I ask are:

- Is the new behavior genuinely useful?
- If it is useful, how will the learner know that?
- Is the new behavior easy to use?
- If it's not easy to use, is there anything that can be done to help that?

DIFFUSIONS OF INNOVATION

The other model I find really useful is from Everett Rogers's classic book *Diffusion of Innovations*. If you haven't read it, you might want to get a copy. It's a really entertaining read, packed with intriguing case studies and loaded with useful stuff. The part I want to focus on here is his take on what perceived attributes affect whether a user adopts or rejects an innovation:

Relative advantage—The degree to which an innovation is perceived as being better than the idea it supersedes

Compatibility—The degree to which an innovation is perceived to be consistent with the existing values, past experiences, and needs of potential adopters

Complexity—The degree to which an innovation is perceived as difficult to use

Observability—The degree to which the results of an innovation are visible to others

Trialability—The opportunity to experiment with the innovation on a limited basis (Rogers 2003)

There is obviously some crossover with TAM, but if I'm designing a learning experience for a new system, I use this as a mental checklist:

- ☐ Are the learners going to believe the new system is better?
- ☐ Are there compatibility issues that need to be addressed?
- ☐ Can we do anything to reduce complexity?
- ☐ Do the learners have a chance to see it being used?
- ☐ Do the learners have a chance to try it out themselves?
- ☐ How can learners have the opportunity to have some success with the new system?

If somebody really, *really* doesn't want to do something, designing instruction around these elements probably isn't going to change their mind. And if a new system, process, or idea is really sucky or a pain in the ass to implement, then it's going to fail no matter how many opportunities you give the learner to try it out.

SELF-EFFICACY

Self-efficacy can be described as someone's belief in their own ability to succeed. Basically, it's the little engine that could ("I think I can...I think I can...").

Earlier in the book, I mentioned a curriculum for drug and alcohol prevention for middle-school students (www.projectalert.com). One of the key elements of that curriculum is developing the students' sense of *resistance self-efficacy.*

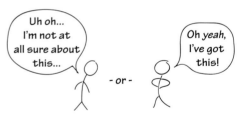

Which of these guys do you think is more likely to try a new method or procedure?

Dealing with peer pressure involving drugs, cigarettes, and alcohol is another classic "I know, but..." scenario, right? For example, kids don't start smoking because they don't know smoking is bad. They've all gotten that message, so there are other reasons. But the situations where students need to make the right decision are emotionally fraught, high-stress situations. Being able to act confidently can make a big difference in those situations.

Students participating in the prevention curriculum practice, and practice more, and practice *more* how they are going to handle the situation. They have statements ready, and they've tried them out in role-play scenarios. Additionally, they have the confidence of their peer group in the class, who have also talked about their strategies in the same circumstances.

In addition to feeling capable, it helps if learners also feel that the necessary task or skill is within their control.

Carol Dweck, a social and developmental psychologist and researcher, conducted an experiment with fifth graders (Mueller & Dweck 1998). She had the students solve a set of problems. When they were done, half the group was told "You must be smart at these problems" and the others were told "You must have worked hard at these problems." She then had students attempt subsequent tasks.

Dweck describes the results:

> We found that praise for intelligence tended to put students in a fixed mind-set (intelligence is fixed, and you have it), whereas praise for effort tended to put them in a growth mind-set (you're developing these skills because you're working hard). We then offered students a chance to work on either a challenging task that they could learn from or an easy one that ensured error-free performance. Most of those praised for intelligence wanted the easy task, whereas most of those praised for effort wanted the challenging task and the opportunity to learn.

When the students tackled subsequent tasks, the students who had been praised for intelligence (something not in their control) did worse than they had done initially, and the students who had been praised for working hard (something they *did* control) did better overall.

Well, that seems to have worked pretty effectively with kids, but are there ways to improve the self-efficacy of adult learners as well?

SCENARIO: MARIANNA (AGAIN)

Let's revisit Marianna, from Chapter 1. You'll recall that she is a newly minted supervisor for her company's IT support department. She was a great IT support person and now she's been promoted, supervising five other IT support workers.

Her HR department has sent her to a new-manager training class, where she learned all about the paperwork necessary for managing hourly workers and about a coaching model for providing good and timely feedback to her direct reports.

Marianna's first few weeks have been a bit rocky. She is swamped by the paperwork demands, and she has to work really hard to keep up. Other supervisors seem to stay on top of their paperwork, so Marianna isn't really sure what she's doing wrong. A couple of her employees are starting to come in late, and she's reluctant to confront them directly about it because she doesn't want to seem as if she got all bossy because she was promoted. She tries to use the coaching method she was taught, but while it works a little with one of the problem employees, it doesn't work at all with the other, and as Marianna gets busy she doesn't finish all the steps to the coaching process. She's not convinced it was helpful anyway.

Marianna's manager is aware that she's struggling somewhat, and is thinking of arranging more managerial training for her.

What are some ways you could design learning experiences that would increase Marianna's sense of self-efficacy?

—TAKE A MOMENT TO CONSIDER WHAT YOU WOULD DO BEFORE MOVING ON—

Practice is a really good place to start, probably first through role-playing with her supervisor or with others who can give her good feedback. She can also shadow some supervisors who are successfully using the coaching model so that she can see it in use. She can try using the coaching model for smaller issues, rather than using it to tackle major performance problems right out of the gate. If she can use it to solve smaller issues, she can gain more confidence in using it with bigger, more intimidating issues. Additionally, she can practice establishing herself as the supervisor of the team by doing activities that are non-punitive—possibly ones around developing the team in positive ways. This will make her more confident in her role as supervisor, which will help when it comes time to deal with more challenging issues.   ■

When fear, anxiety, or discomfort with the new behavior has been identified as one of the main issues, practice becomes particularly important.

In the handwashing example, we identified talking to another colleague about their lack of hand hygiene as a problematic behavior. Nobody really wants to have that awkward conversation with a colleague.

It's likely that the only way a health care professional would get past the discomfort of that conversation is through practice. Just like the kids in the Project ALERT classes who had to practice how they were going handle an offer of cigarettes or alcohol, health care staff probably need to practice how they will gently remind a colleague that they might want to use some hand gel before examining a patient.

MODELING AND PRACTICE

In Marianna's example, we looked at the value of observing someone else and of practicing to develop self-efficacy.

These practices have benefits besides developing self-efficacy. We know that the elephant is a creature of habit, and that it likes to learn from its direct experience (remember the second driver in the texting example?).

Well-worn path

It takes effort to switch paths. By creating opportunities for the learner to see behaviors modeled and to practice them, you greatly increase the likelihood that those behaviors will continue later.

Another way to practice and to increase the likelihood of a behavior being used is to walk learners a few steps down the path as part of the learning design. By this I mean to have your learners prepare themselves to employ the knowledge or skill by actively figuring out how they will use it to address their own specific challenges or tasks—stick with them as they think through moving from the theoretical to the practical.

We've talked a lot about using scenarios to make learning more vivid and engaging, but the best scenarios are the learner's actual problems or challenges.

Here are some examples:

Topic	Design
How to write better performance reviews	Have learners bring to class a performance review that they need to write. Structure activities and discussions around writing that review. At the end of the class, each learner will have a draft of a real performance review.
Filling out tax returns	Have students start their own returns.
Speaking Thai	Have learners think about things they'd like to be able to talk about (their kids, music, food, politics, introducing themselves), and have them work on ways to talk about those topics in Thai.
Project management	Have learners bring their own project documents and project concerns, and be ready to discuss those concerns. Have them work on solutions to those problems as part of the class.

This set of tactics does a few useful things. First, it gets the learners imagining how they can use the material in their own world. They start picturing the possibilities and figuring out how to deal with obstacles.

Second, it lets the learner get some practice with their own material when there is still support to iron out snags.

Third, the learners have now made an investment. Behavioral economists talk about *sunk cost* and loss aversion. People have a strong reluctance to discard something that they've already invested in.

Fourth, they are ready to go when they get back to the real world. There's always a barrier to starting something new, and if the learner has already scaled part of that barrier, then there's less effort required from them as they continue.

So whenever it's feasible, have learners apply the subject matter to their own situations.

SOCIAL PROOF

We've already talked about how a good way to attract an elephant's attention is to tell it that all the other elephants are doing it.

But social proof (as discussed in Chapter 5—you remember, the tendency of people to base their own actions on the actions of others around them) is not only useful for attracting attention. It's also really good for encouraging the behavior.

Additionally, we can't be experts on everything, so a good tool—often an effective shortcut—is to turn to or cite people whose opinions we respect and whose advice we seek. If those people tell us that something is useful, we are much more likely to try it ourselves. I have folks who, if they tell me to go check something out, I'll do it without much question because I trust their opinion.

I've worked on a number of client projects where, at the beginning of the course, there has been a "this is a really important initiative" message from the CEO or the relevant vice president, which is fine. It's good to know that a project is known and supported at the top—it gives it a feeling of authority, I guess you'd say.

But really, who is, or should be, the actual authority figure when it comes to doing your job? Is it the CEO, or is it the person in the next cubicle who has five times as much experience as you? If you are shopping on Amazon, whose opinion are you going to really value—the publisher, whose blurb assures you this author is a GENIUS, or the 19 readers who said "meh"?

In the Project ALERT drug-prevention project, they use influential opinion leaders to talk to kids about reasons not to do drugs. Granted, the term "influential opinion leaders" means different things in different situations, but if you are a 13-year-old school kid, whose opinion would you most value?

Parents?   Teachers?   Police officers?   16-year-olds?

Obviously, that depends on the 13-year-old, but as a general rule, for middle schoolers, high school kids are pretty much the arbiters of what is and is not cool. To that end, Project ALERT doesn't spend a lot of time on lectures from adult authority figures, but they make good use of teenagers talking about their experiences and about how to make good choices.

So think about it—given your subject matter, who are the really influential people in your organization or in the eyes of your target audience? How can you make those opinions visible? Here are a few possibilities:

- **Have people describe successes with the process, procedure, or skill.** These descriptions can be presented on an intranet, on a discussion forum, in email blasts, or through any delivery methods already available in an organization. If possible, you could create mini feature stories about the person who is using the process to good effect—that person could be the star of the show.

- **Engage opinion leaders first.** Involve your opinion leaders in the planning of the endeavor and in the creation and design of the learning experience. Can you have them lend case studies, or agree to champion the undertaking? Can you have them mentor others?
- **Make progress visible.** Many games put up leaderboards to show who is really killing it. While shaming low-performing people publicly is counter-productive, having a way to acknowledge those who are succeeding can encourage others.

VISCERAL MATTERS

The elephant is not influenced only by outside forces like peer encouragement. The elephant is also swayed by direct experience and strong emotion. Direct visual choices and visceral experiences can sway the choices that learners make.

For example, in the cake-or-fruit-salad choice from Chapter 5, people were more likely to pick the cake if it was actually in front of them. When the choice was more abstract, they had more self-control about choosing fruit salad.

Thinking back to our texting-while-driving issue, how could we make the experience more visceral or direct for people?

Here are a couple of ways this has been done:

- *The New York Times* created an interactive game that tests how good you are at changing lanes while distracted by a text message. It measures how much your reaction time slows down when you are trying to deal with distractions. You get direct experience with your own limitations. Unfortunately, it's not a very realistic simulation (you change lanes by pressing numbers on the keyboard).
- In 2009, the Gwent police force, in Wales, sponsored the creation of a video showing teenage girls in a car. The driver is texting, and while she does, the car drifts across the median line and strikes an oncoming car. A horrific accident ensues, and you see every graphic detail.

These are both visceral procedures—one involving direct experience and one an emotionally wrenching video. There's no data I can find on the outcome of either solution, unfortunately. However, I can tell you from experience that I do flash on the memory of the video if I'm ever tempted to break my own rule against texting while driving.

While scare tactics often fail to change behavior, there does seem to be some benefit to strong visceral experiences, although more research is needed in this area.

YOU NEED TO FOLLOW UP

All of the above suggestions and strategies can be useful, but possibly the most important idea to keep in mind is this:

> **CHANGE IS A PROCESS, NOT AN EVENT:** Any time you want learners to change their behavior, it's a process and *it needs to be reinforced.*

The ways to reinforce the change are all the things we've already discussed, so this isn't a new idea at this point, but it's still an important point. Be patient! Even if all your learners start out with the best intentions and are making a conscious effort to implement the new solution or innovation, they are likely to trickle off if the change isn't reinforced. Always consider how that change will be reinforced over the long term.

SUMMARY

- There are two kinds of motivation that learning designers need to consider: motivation to learn and motivation to do.
- When you hear "I know, but...," that's a clue that you'll probably need to design for motivation.
- "I know, but..." frequently comes up when there is a delayed reward or consequence.
- We learn from experience, but it can be a problem if we learn the *wrong thing* from experience.
- Lack of visible feedback or consequences is one of the most common attributes of a motivation challenge.
- We are creatures of habit—irritating for the short-term learning curve but potentially useful if we can help learners develop a new habit.

- You may be able to influence your learners, but you can't control them.
- Learning designs should show the learners how something new is useful and easy to use.
- Try to ensure that your learners get the opportunity to observe and try new processes or procedures.
- Learners need to feel a sense of self-efficacy with the new challenge or skill.
- Learners may need to practice uncomfortable or difficult behaviors until they can overcome anxiety and feel confident.
- Use opinion leaders as examples.
- Visceral experiences may have more impact than abstract ones, although the research on this topic is ongoing.
- Change is a process, not an event.

REFERENCES

Bandura, Albert. 1977. "Self-efficacy: Toward a Unifying Theory of Behavioral Change." *Psychological Review* 84: 191–215.

Dance, Gabriel, Tom Jackson, and Aron Pilhofer. 2009. "Gauging Your Distraction." *New York Times*. www.nytimes.com/interactive/2009/07/19/technology/20090719-driving-game.html.

Davis, F. D. 1989. "Perceived Usefulness, Perceived Ease of Use, and User Acceptance of Information Technology." *MIS Quarterly* 13(3): 319–340.

Dweck, Carol S. 2007. "The Perils and Promises of Praise." *Educational Leadership* 65 (2): 34–39.

Fogg, BJ. 2011, 2010. Behavior Model (www.behaviormodel.org) and Behavior Grid (www.behaviorgrid.org).

Mueller, Claudia M. and Carol S. Dweck. 1998. "Intelligence Praise Can Undermine Motivation and Performance." *Journal of Personality and Social Psychology* 75: 33–52.

PSA Texting and Driving, U.K. 2009. www.youtube.com/watch?v=8I54mlK0kVw. Described at www.gwent.police.uk/leadnews.php?a=2172.

Rogers, Everett M. 2003. *Diffusion of Innovations (5th edition)*. Glencoe: Free Press.

DESIGN FOR HABITS

(IN WHICH WE LEARN THE IMPORTANCE OF
PROVIDING THE ELEPHANT WITH A PLAN
AND A WELL-WORN PATH)

WHAT IS A HABIT?

A habit is defined as "an acquired behavior pattern regularly followed until it has become almost involuntary."

We all have a general sense of what habits are, but let's take a look at how habits can be part of proficiency.

THE STORY OF TWO PROJECT MANAGERS

Linda and An Mei are project managers for a software development company.

Both of them are certified Project Management Professionals (PMPs), and both have been project managers for several years. And both are having a challenging week. Take a look at how they responded to some of the daily challenges in being a project manager.

Challenge: A contractor is claiming he didn't know the due date for a deliverable.

Linda   An Mei

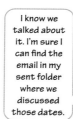 I know we talked about it. I'm sure I can find the email in my sent folder where we discussed those dates.

He knows. Whenever I update the schedule, I require a signoff from each team member.

Challenge: Developers coming late to a meeting.

It's a headache, isn't it? But I understand how it happens, and if I try to start without everyone, I just end up repeating myself.

It doesn't happen to me too often, because people learn pretty quickly that I start my meetings right on time.

Challenge: A client needs an update to an old project.

The developer who worked on that project quit last month. We are checking who has all her files.

I archive a full version of the project after each major phase. The final version is archived on the server.

The difference between An Mei and Linda isn't necessarily knowledge. Both project managers have mastered the practice of project management well enough to pass the PMP exam, which is not an easy test.

The difference between them seems to be more about their habits of communication, organization, and vigilance. That's certainly been my experience working with project managers.

So how does habit design intersect with learning design? If good habits are crucial for success, then how do we help support the development of those habits?

THE ANATOMY OF A HABIT

So we looked at the definition of a habit ("an acquired behavior pattern regularly followed until it has become almost involuntary"), but it may be useful to break that down a bit more.

- **An acquired behavior pattern.** We typically need to learn the behavior that we want to make a habit. We aren't born with an instinctive desire to floss our teeth, for example; it's something we need to learn. Like many habits, though, flossing isn't a particularly complicated behavior to learn. It's pretty simple, and there isn't a lot of art to it. But it's clear that teaching someone to floss isn't going to magically transform them into a daily flosser. So learning the habit may be a necessary but not sufficient condition for acquiring the habit.

- **Triggers.** Most models of habit acquisition involve identifying the trigger that activates the habit. It could be a trigger that you are arbitrarily attaching to the new behavior ("When I get my first cup of coffee in the morning, I will take my vitamins"), or it could be a trigger that naturally occurs in in the course of daily life ("When one of my direct reports emails me a deliverable, I will take a few minutes to give them feedback"). An "almost involuntary" behavior needs to have something that activates it. BJ Fogg, of the Persuasive Technology Lab at Stanford, has triggers as a key part of his behavior model (behavior = motivation + ability + trigger).

- **Motivation.** All the motivation issues discussed in Chapter 8 apply here, autonomy in particular. No one can be *told* a habit. A habit may be a requirement of someone's job, and a required action over time can become automatic, but many desirable workplace habits are only going to become routine if the person is actively motivated, which means that that person needs to have autonomy and control over the process. And motivation alone does not mean a habit will be formed, or everyone would still be using that gym membership they got after New Year's.

- **Feedback.** The most difficult habits to acquire are frequently the ones that lack any visible feedback. In his book *The Power of Habit*, Charles Duhigg talks about how the addition of substances like citric acid and mint oil to Pepsodent created a tingly clean feeling that reinforced the action of brushing (despite the fact that the tingly compounds don't actually impact cleanliness). Habits for which the feedback is delayed or absent are frequently the hardest habits to acquire. For example, unless you are fortunate enough to get an immediate endorphin rush from the act of exercise, it may be weeks or months before you start to see the benefits of daily jogging. It's difficult to persist in an activity with no visible benefit, so most people starting an exercise program will attempt to measure or quantify their progress in some way. Fitness trackers such as the Fitbit are a way to ensure that you can see progress much more quickly.

- **Practice or Repetition.** Using our definition, something can't be classified as a habit until it's "regularly followed until it has become almost involuntary." We've probably all heard metrics for how long it takes to acquire a habit—seven times, or twenty-one days—but unfortunately the real answer is that it depends. It depends on the complexity and difficulty of the behavior, on the mechanisms set up to support it, on the presence of feedback, and on the motivation of the person forming the habit.

- **Environment.** One of the other determiners of habit formation is how well the environment supports the habit. We'll discuss this further in Chapter 11, but if I'm trying to acquire the habit of flossing, I dramatically improve the likelihood that I'll floss if I have a ready supply of dental floss at the necessary time and place. A supportive environment can also include creating social supports—for example, an exercise partner or someone you report back to who keeps you accountable. Breaking an undesirable habit can involve removing the triggers from the environment.

A friend wanted to break the habit of spending too much time on her smartphone before bed. She found herself staying up later and later because of the digital distraction. She could keep the phone out of the bedroom altogether (in the same way that some people trying to break the habit of distracted driving start putting their phones in the trunk when they drive somewhere), but she had family members who would sometimes need to reach her at night, so she wanted to be able to hear the phone ring. She settled on putting the phone in box on her bedside table—it was close enough to hear, but because she didn't have the visual trigger of the phone, she was much less likely to idly pick it up and get distracted when she went to bed.

THE BENEFITS OF AUTOMATICITY

One factor that we've mentioned repeatedly is automaticity. Our definition uses the phrase "until it has become almost involuntary."

Without automaticity—you can do it without really thinking about it—you don't really have a habit. All those terms (automatic, unconscious, involuntary) are terms we associate with the elephant.

Well-worn path

When you are first acquiring a habit, you are relying on willpower to make it happen. If it's a particularly strenuous habit, you may need to use a lot of will-power, but if you can persist, it becomes easier as it becomes more automatic.

If it becomes automatic enough, it actually becomes easier to do it than to not do it. An example of this is seat belts.

Are you a regular seat belt wearer? If you aren't you probably should be, right?

But if you are a regular seat belt wearer, what happens when you don't wear one? For example, have you ever needed to move a car a small distance, maybe to a different parking space, and you don't wear your seat belt? There's no danger— you aren't going to exceed five miles an hour, there are no other cars or obstacles of any kind—but it doesn't *feel* right. It's essentially impossible to be in jeopardy, but it still feels twitchy and uncomfortable to not put your seat belt on.

If you are not a driver, then there may be some other equivalent—say, when you need to get off the bus or train a stop later than usual, or when you deviate from your morning routine.

Whenever you are deciding to act or not act, you are balancing the effort of action against the potential benefit of that action. Putting on your seat belt clearly has benefit, but it's an infrequent benefit; you might put your seat belt on a thousand times before anything happens that actually necessitates the seat belt. If you had to consciously exert willpower every time you put your seat belt on—if it were essentially the same amount of effort the thousandth time as it was the first time—it would be difficult to keep doing it in the absence of visible benefit, but making it a habit reduces the effort necessary to repeat the action. After putting on your seat belt becomes automatic, the effort to do it is very, very small.

IDENTIFYING HABIT GAPS

So how do you know the difference between something that is a procedure or a skill and something that is a habit? The answer is that there is probably overlap between those categories, but conscious effort and automaticity are probably the main criteria to look at.

Many habits may not require much skill. My dental hygienist could explain the skill behind flossing, but the subtlety is lost on me. As far as I'm concerned, it's a procedural task but not much of a skill. So if I'm not flossing regularly, the gap isn't my ability to floss, but rather because I lack the habit. I need to figure out how make flossing an automatic behavior that doesn't require a lot of conscious effort.

> **IDENTIFY THE HABIT:** Does it need to be done automatically and without concious effort?

But what if the gap is not so clear-cut? Many behavior gaps could require an overlap of skill development and habit formation.

> **OVERLAP:** A habit can be based on what was begun as a learned skill.

I had a job in college doing data entry for loan applications. Loan applications have a lot of numbers, and I got pretty used to using the 10-key pad on my keyboard:

10-key pad

Even today, if I need to enter numbers, it's much more natural for me to use the 10-key pad, and if I'm on a laptop without one, I find it incredibly awkward.

I wouldn't have acquired that habit without first learning to use a 10-key pad (a skill, requiring practice), but now that skill is also a habit. I *automatically* use a 10-key pad when it's available, without really thinking about it or making a conscious decision.

These are both simple, self-contained examples. Let's take a look at a more complex behavior, and what parts of it are habits. Let's talk about time management.

EXAMPLE: TIME MANAGEMENT

Everyone agrees that time management is a crucial skill that we need in both our personal and professional lives, but let's focus on time management for work. Is time management a habit?

In and of itself, time management is too big a set of behaviors to be a habit, but it *contains* several habits.

Francis Wade, in his book *Perfect Time-Based Productivity*, identified that time management, rather than being a few small behaviors, is a series of large behaviors (e.g., capturing, emptying, tossing, acting, storing, etc.) that are composed of several smaller behaviors.

He defines *capturing* as "the process of storing time demands (e.g., tasks or to-do items) in a safe place for later retrieval and processing." Basically, how do you track all the things you need to do?

Time management is something I struggle with. Some of my to-do items are in my email inbox, some are scribbled on notes stuck to my computer monitor, some are in meeting notes in my notebook, some are in my actual to-do application, and some are (unfortunately) just in my memory.

Some of the habits Wade identified for a better method include:

- **Carrying a manual capture point (other than memory) at all times.** Basically, this is the habit of always having a way to write down the things you need to do. It could be a notebook, a smartphone app, a voice recorder, or whatever works for you, but the first habit is just making sure you always have it with you.
- **Capturing manually.** This second habit is actually *using* your capture device (not just remembering to take it with you). It's actually writing things down in your notebook or adding things to your smartphone app.

- **Consolidating things from automatic capture points.** This involves pulling tasks or to-dos from other places (email, text messages, etc.) into your main capture device, rather than having tasks in several different places.

None of these items requires a high degree of skill or a steep learning curve. They are all simple behaviors. But getting them to be a regular part of your time management practice really does require making them automatic *habits*.

CONTEXT AND TRIGGERS

The context and triggers for each of these habits are a little different. For example, the context for the first behavior (carrying a manual capture point) is getting ready for work in the morning or getting ready to leave the office.

Trigger	Behavior
Getting ready to leave	Checking that I have my notebook

The context for the second behavior (capturing manually) is a little different. The triggers there might be someone asking you to do something, or you thinking of something you want or should do.

Perceived Usefulness	Perceived Ease of Use
Someone has a request	Record the request in my notebook
I think of a to-do	Record the to-do in my notebook

This makes the second habit a little more complicated, as the contexts are a little less predictable. To-do items could happen during a meeting, during a hallway conversation, on a phone call, or anywhere you just happen to think of something. Because the triggers can be so much more variable, the ability to recognize the trigger and the need to create an automatic association between the trigger and the behavior become all the more important.

QUESTIONS TO ASK

Some of the questions you can ask to identify and understand habit gaps are:

- Is this something that people need to do consistently and automatically?
- If I break this behavior down to its smaller components, do habits become visible?
- What is the specific context or trigger that is involved?

- Do those triggers occur at variable or unpredictable times?
- Is this something that isn't automatically part of a larger process?
- Is there an undesirable habit that needs to be undone first?

DESIGNING FOR HABIT

So what are some of the solutions that can be applied to habit formation? The science is still developing around this question, actually. The healthcare industry, in particular, is looking closely at habit design because dealing with many of the most expensive health conditions relies on consistent healthy (habitual) behaviors. Researchers at Stanford and MIT are trying to decode the behaviors and brain functions behind habit formation.

The software industry is paying attention as well. Habit formation is being studied by software designers who would love for their new app to become a regular part of your day. Apps are also being designed to help you develop your own habits, whether you are trying eat better, manage your inbox, or avoid distractions.

Although the science around habit formation is still forming, some strategies have been identified.

IMPLEMENTATION INTENTIONS

The academic and researcher Peter Gollwitzer spends a lot of time on the idea of *implementation intentions*. He explains them as follows:

> *Implementation intentions are if-then plans that connect anticipated critical situations with responses that will be effective in accomplishing one's goals. Whereas...goals specify what one wants to do/achieve (i.e., "I intend to perform behavior X!"...), implementation intentions specify the behavior that one will perform in the service of goal achievement if the anticipated critical situation is actually encountered (i.e., "If situation Y occurs, then I will initiate goal-directed behavior Z!").*

So if you are trying to quit smoking, you need more than the goal ("I'm going to stop smoking")—you need the implementation intention of how to actually do it.

So you could say:

If I get a craving, I will distract myself.

You have situation Y ("If I get a craving") and behavior Z ("I will distract myself"). This is more effective than just the goal ("I will quit smoking"). But you can make it much more effective by being specific:

If I crave a cigarette when I'm stressed out, I will call my sister.

If I crave a cigarette when I'm bored, I'll play that candy game on my phone.

If I crave a cigarette because it's after lunch, I will take a 5-minute walk outside.

If I crave a cigarette because I'm in a social situation, I'll chew gum.

It turns out that deciding how to handle a fraught situation requires a lot of effort, and exerting willpower also requires a lot of effort, according to the psychologist and researcher Roy Baumeister. If you make the decision ahead of time ("If Y happens, I will do Z"), then the action is clear and you have more cognitive resources to apply to taking the action.

As part of a learning experience you can have people identify their own anticipated critical situations, and have a specific behavioral strategy for responding ("When I have problem X with my difficult employee, I will do Y"). Have people create their own implementation intentions and remember that specificity is crucial to success.

SHRINK THE HABIT

If a habit seems overwhelming, make it smaller. Both Chip and Dan Heath (in their excellent book *Switch*) and BJ Fogg, in his Tiny Habits program, discuss the importance of identifying the smallest productive behavior and focusing on that.

We talked about how making a behavior habitual makes it easier to do, but if the behavior is too effortful to be established as a habit, is there a way you can make it smaller and more manageable?

For example, if you want to develop the habit of regularly getting up and stretching at your desk so that you don't sit too long, it's probably best not to start with a full set of yoga poses as you try to build your habit. Instead, could you stand up and reach your arms up once? Or even just stand up? Eventually, if that becomes a habit, you can add more behaviors to the established habit, which is easier than creating a whole new habit. If you are overwhelmed by the big behavior, what's a small behavior you can do?

PRACTICE AND FEEDBACK

The most obvious solutions are in some ways the most challenging: practice and feedback.

As we mentioned when discussing motivation in Chapter 8, the hardest behaviors to acquire are the ones in which there's no visible feedback.

In Francis Wade's time management example, he recognized that time management frequently feels intangible. Although you recognize the impact of poor time management overall, the specific behavior is often without immediate consequence. If you forget to write down a task, the impact of that isn't felt for quite a while, long after the behavior has failed to occur.

To make things more visible, Wade created a level system (using the same belt colors as are used in martial arts) to make time management behaviors more visible. Each behavior has a self-diagnosis rubric to help people identify where they are with their time management habits:

CAPTURING CHEAT-SHEET

BEHAVIOR	WHITE	YELLOW	ORANGE	GREEN
Carry a manual Capture Point at all times	Rarely or never ☐	Sometimes ☐	Often ☐	Almost always ☐
Use a manual Capture Point instead of memory	Rarely or never ☐	Sometimes ☐	Often ☐	Always ☐
Consolidate automatic Capture Points		Starting ☐	Occasional ☐	Sustained ☐
Maintain a flexible backup method		Starting ☐	Sometimes in place ☐	Always in place ☐
Current Belt	☐	☐	☐	☐

From Francis Wade's *Perfect Time-Based Productivity.* Used with permission.

This is the same logic that underlies many of the "quantified self" gadgets—the fitness trackers, food diaries, and habit reminder apps. How can we make behaviors more visible and reinforce practice?

REDUCE THE BARRIERS

A key question to ask when thinking about design for habits is, "Is there any way to make the behavior easier?" That is, is there anything you can do to reduce the barriers to performance?

I live in a place where winter goes on for a long time, and it's hard to get enough sun exposure in the winter months. My doctor recommended a vitamin D supplement, which I was bad at remembering to take.

The way I was finally successful was by chaining the vitamin-taking behavior to an existing behavior that I had no problem with: my morning coffee habit.

I work from home, and one of my first actions most mornings is to make a cup of coffee. This usually involves a few minutes of lingering around the kitchen while the water boils. If I put the vitamin D container next to the coffee jar, it became *much* easier to remember to take the vitamin. In fact, the empty time waiting for the water to boil meant that taking the vitamin was as close to effortless as possible. This chains the new habit to an existing habit.

APPLYING TO LEARNING DESIGN

So how do you build any of this into a learning design? A few possibilities include:

- **Have learners create implementation intentions.** Give learners an opportunity, or even a template, that allows them to create their own implementation intentions (*"If x happens, I will do y"*).
- **Introduce the habit, and allow learners to brainstorm solutions.** Present learners with the goal, and allow them to work on how to accomplish it.
- **Carve out time for specific habits.** If you are trying to develop habits, it can be useful to spread them out over time and then reinforce that. For example, if a healthcare facility wants its staff to develop some new habits, they could introduce one very small habit at the beginning of each month, and have a fun campaign about working on that single habit for the first week of the month, with a few follow-ups later in the month. That way, there's sufficient time for a habit to develop.
- **Reduce the barriers.** Identify ways you can reduce the barriers and, even more importantly, give learners the opportunity to think about how they can reduce the barriers for themselves.

- **Create rubrics or tracking mechanisms.** Figure out what you can do to make the habit more visible.
- **Help tie the habit to an existing behavior.** Help learners identify an existing behavior they can chain the new habit to.
- **Hack the environment.** Have learners survey their environment and figure out how they can modify it to support habit development.
- **Identify the triggers.** Give learners the assignment of observing and noting triggers in their own environment for a few days, and then have them report back. They can practice the activity of looking for triggers before they start adding in the behavior.

ONE LAST WORD ON AUTONOMY AND CONTROL

In all learning activities, it's important to give the learner control over their own learning whenever possible, but it's particularly important for habit development.

It's worth reiterating that you can't *tell* someone a habit. As we all know, habits we *want* to develop are hard enough. Habits we are reluctantly being coerced into are almost certainly going to fail.

Some habits aren't optional. Hand-washing for healthcare workers isn't really optional, but how that habit is best developed can be.

SUMMARY

- Habits are "an acquired behavior pattern regularly followed until it has become almost involuntary."
- The difference between weak and strong performance can come down to habits, even when knowledge, skills, and motivation are already present.
- Habit formation requires being able to identify the triggers for that habit, and having a plan in place to respond to those triggers.
- No one can be *told* a habit. People need to participate in habit formation.
- Habit formation usually requires practice and feedback.
- Hacking the environment, shrinking the habit, and chaining a new habit to an existing behavior can increase the likelihood of the habit being formed.

REFERENCES

Bandura, Albert. 1977. "Self-efficacy: Toward a Unifying Theory of Behavioral Change." *Psychological Review* 84: 191-215.

Baumeister, Roy and John Tierney. 2012.*Willpower: Rediscovering the Greatest Human Strength*. Penguin Books.

Duhigg, Charles. 2014. *The Power of Habit: Why We Do What We Do in Life and Business.* New York: Random House.

Fogg, BJ. "The Fogg Behavior Model." Retrieved May 05, 2015, from www.behaviormodel.org.

Habit. (n.d.). Dictionary.com Unabridged. Retrieved May 05, 2015, from http://dictionary.reference.com/browse/habit.

Heath, Chip and Dan. 2010. *Switch: How to Change Things When Change Is Hard.* Crown Business.

Kahneman, Daniel. 2011. *Thinking, Fast and Slow*. Farrar, Straus, and Giroux.

PSA Texting and Driving, U.K. 2009. www.youtube.com/watch?v=8I54mIK0kVw. Described at www.gwent.police.uk/leadnews.php?a=2172.

Rainforest Alliance, "Follow the Frogs." www.rainforest-alliance.org.

Rubin, Gretchen. 2015. *Better than Before: Mastering the Habits of Our Everyday Lives.* New York: Crown Publishers.

Wade, Francis. 2014. "Perfect Time-Based Productivity: A Unique Way to Protect Your Peace of Mind as Time Demands Increase." Framework Consulting Inc. / 2Time Labs.

SOCIAL AND INFORMAL LEARNING

(IN WHICH WE LEARN THAT LEARNING DOESN'T FOLLOW A STRAIGHT LINE, AND THAT SOMETIMES IT IS ALL ABOUT WHO YOU KNOW)

WHAT DOES LEARNING LOOK LIKE IN YOUR ORGANIZATION?

When I was getting ready to write this chapter, I talked to a few colleagues who know a lot about social and informal learning.

One of them, Mark Britz, an organizational performance strategist who specializes in social and informal learning, said:

> If you took a picture of your organization and looked at where learning was happening, it wouldn't just be in the classroom.

Jane Bozarth demonstrated this beautifully in her book *Show Your Work*, where she featured a teacher-created Pinterest board called "What does learning look like?" Almost all the images are of people *doing* things, rather than images of traditional classrooms (Bozarth 2014).

So let's try this for ourselves. Imagine we took a picture of your organization or workplace:

Your first reaction would probably be, "Wow, what an attractive, well-dressed, and diverse bunch of co-workers I have! They could be in a stock photo!"

But after you finish admiring your remarkably photogenic colleagues, you could look at how learning is happening:

- One of your co-workers is getting advice from another co-worker about his client proposal.
- Another colleague is showing a junior colleague how to perform a new task for which she's going to be responsible.
- Somebody pinned an interesting article to the bulletin board, or posted the article to an internal discussion forum.
- Somebody is reading their Twitter feed to see what their broader professional network is talking about today.
- Someone else is Googling how to save their presentation in a format that can be read on a mobile device.

These are all examples of informal or social learning.

> **INFORMAL OR SOCIAL LEARNING:** Encompasses pretty much any learning that happens outside a formal learning event such as a classroom or an elearning course.

This is what Jay Cross refers to as "the unofficial, unscheduled, impromptu way people learn to do their jobs" in his book *Informal Learning*.

A number of different definitions exist for social learning. Marcia Conner and Tony Bingham, in their book *The New Social Learning*, define it as "participating with others to make sense of new ideas." Other definitions focus on learning from observing others' behaviors, or using social media to connect people into learning networks (often referred to as PLNs, or personal learning networks).

This chapter will take a look at some of the ways informal and social learning are parts of the learner's journey.

IT'S NOT A STRAIGHT LINE

When I think about designing a learning experience, I try to always think beyond the initial learning event(s). I try to consider all of the following:

- **Learning.** How is the initial learning event structured?
- **Practice.** How does the learner get practice and hands-on, visceral experience?
- **Feedback.** How does the learner get feedback on their performance? How are they getting coaching or mentoring?
- **Support.** How does the learner access resources at a moment of need? How do they get help troubleshooting?
- **Refreshing.** If it's an infrequently used skill or procedure, how is it being refreshed or reinforced? How are we using spacing to make the knowledge more durable?
- **Developing Further.** If it's a complex skill, how is the learner getting to the next level? How can the learner continue to develop skills and move toward mastery?

This is a journey that will inevitably have formal, informal, and social components.

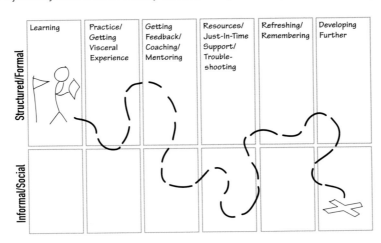

So let's take a look at how this can work.

BALANCING FORMAL AND INFORMAL

So what's the best option? Formal? Informal? Social? The answer is, of course, it depends. They all have their place. There are a few factors that may influence the solutions that you invest in:

- **Tacit versus explicit.** Formal learning experiences are usually about communicating explicit rule sets. For example, a complicated procedure that requires practice might be a good candidate for a formal learning experience. Topics that are mostly tacit are more difficult to make into formal learning, except as case studies or role-plays.
- **Complexity.** Highly complex topics can be difficult to reduce into formal learning experiences. When they are turned into formal learning, the subject matter can often only be an explanation of general principles, rather than prescriptive behaviors. For example, you might learn several good principles of salary negotiation in a career seminar, but when applying those principles in a specific situation you may need to use informal or social learning (e.g., talk it over with a mentor or a colleague) to help you decide what to do.
- **Changeability of the material.** Formal learning experiences often take a while to develop, and it's difficult to develop formal learning around volatile, changeable subject matter. For example, I deliberately limited the number of references to particular learning technologies in this book because the technology landscape changes very quickly, and it's easy for that information to go out of date. Informal or social learning can often be more flexible and a better source of up-to-date information.

Sometimes formal learning isn't necessary because it's overkill. You need to ask, "What is really necessary to support performance?" For example, a formal learning class on how to use the company's uncomplicated voicemail system is just a creative form of torture for all involved. A quick job aid will support the needed performance and will be much more pleasant for everyone involved.

So let's take a look at an example to see what combination of formal, informal and social learning would be most effective.

HIRO'S JOURNEY

Meet Hiro.

He's a new associate for an architectural design firm. He needs to learn how to budget projects.

Hiro has five goals with respect to learning to budget projects:

- **Goal 1:** Enter budget data into the software that the firm uses to estimate projects.
- **Goal 2:** Construct complete budgets that encompass all the likely project costs.
- **Goal 3:** Recognize whether a budget has any risky areas that could cause the company to lose money.
- **Goal 4:** Manage budgets throughout the project, and troubleshoot cost overruns that may occur.
- **Goal 5:** Continually develop project management skills regarding budget and cost controls.

For each of these goals, we'll look at the balance between formal and informal/ social solutions, and at some of the tools that can be used to promote social or informal learning:

- Performance support and just-in-time resources
- Mentoring and apprenticeship programs
- Social learning communities
- Working out loud, and reflective activities
- Curation
- Social networking

GOAL 1: LEARN THE SOFTWARE

The first thing that Hiro needs to learn is to enter budget data into the computer system that the firm uses to estimate projects.

If we use our criteria to evaluate this learning goal, would formal learning make sense? The gap here is primarily knowledge of the software procedures, so the material is pretty explicit and not overly complex. This particular system has enough complication that a class of some kind would probably be helpful, but it would also be good to support it with appropriate just-in-time resources such as job aids or short video recordings of how to perform certain tasks. Additionally, it's likely that Hiro will still need social support in the form of knowing who to ask or where on the company intranet he can post if he has a question.

Formal	Informal	Social
Hiro takes an elearning course to learn the basic function of the software.	Hiro accesses job aids and resources as needed.	Hiro knows who to ask if he has problems.

Tool: Just-In-Time Resources

We'll take another look at job aids in Chapter 11, but a good pool of accessible resources is often more useful than a formal course. Those resources can include job aids, videos, wiki entries, or forum posts. The resources can be official job aids, or they can be a collection of helpful tips pulled from the community. They don't have to be beautiful; they just have to be useful. If you Google "how to knit" you'll likely wind up on YouTube watching an amateur video filmed with somebody's phone. And that's perfect if it helps you get started—the production values won't matter if it's clear, easy to understand, and helpful. Often the best way to maintain these resources is to have the community revise existing ones and generate new ones. For example, if Hiro figures out a good way to visualize his budget data, he could add that to the company's knowledge base about the software.

GOAL 2: CONSTRUCT GOOD BUDGETS

Hiro's second goal is to construct complete budgets that encompass all the likely project costs.

The gaps here are more related to knowledge, procedures, and skills. This is a more complex topic, and it requires that Hiro understand the difference between estimating costs for a home kitchen remodel and estimating costs for the construction of a commercial building. Improperly constructed budgets could cost the company a lot of money, so it's in their interest to make sure Hiro can do this properly.

The balance of formal, informal, and social is probably a bit different here. Formal learning has a role to play, but Hiro's work will probably need to be supervised for a while before he can operate independently. Formal learning can teach him all the steps in the process and give him some practice, but there are a lot of subtleties that he'll learn only through experience. After training, his company puts him on small-budget projects and makes sure he has a mentor.

Formal	Informal / Social
Hiro takes a two-day class on budgeting, where he works through case examples.	Hiro starts with small budget projects, and is assigned to Mila, a mentor in the company. She has some formal milestones, including scheduled budget reviews with Hiro and his manager, but she also acts as an informal resource when he has questions or needs help.

Tool: Coaching, Mentoring, or Apprenticeship Programs

Often, complex skills require practice over time. The best training class in the world can get learners only so far, and after that they need to practice, try things, get feedback, and repeat. Coaching, mentoring, and apprenticeship programs are a form of social learning that can be used for complex skills. Some such programs are highly formalized, like some student-teacher training programs or apprenticeship programs for building trades. Others are more informal. Learners may be matched with mentors with no formal requirements, or they may seek out unofficial coaches that answer questions, give advice, or review work.

GOAL 3: IDENTIFY PITFALLS

Hiro's next goal is to recognize whether a budget has any risky areas that could cause the company to lose money. The company has taken a big loss on a few previous budgets, so this is a sensitive topic. The problem is that this is a really hard thing to teach. The experienced people know how to spot potential problem areas, but most of them learned it the hard way—through painful experience. When they try to explain exactly how to identify the issues, the characteristics are hard to quantify and sometimes contradict each other. The subject matter experts often resort to phrases like "You know it when you see it" and "Well, it just depends." Hiro can ask Mila for help, and she can spot most issues, but even her experience doesn't cover all examples.

Tool: Working Out Loud

Jane Bozarth's book *Show Your Work: The Payoffs and How-to's of Working Out Loud* is an excellent primer for encouraging knowledge and experience sharing. As soon as the knowledge starts being transformed from a specific visible example to an abstract "best practice," crucial details and important context start to get edited out.

She explains that "knowing *what* gets done is not the same as knowing *how* it gets done."

For example, business books are full of good advice, but reading a recommendation like "product brands should use social media to engage authentically with their customers" is one thing, and seeing that an airline Tweets out the homeward journey of a lost pet or that a fast food chain features real-life fans on its Facebook page is another. And getting to peek behind the curtain to understand how and why they chose to feature those particular examples is even better, particularly if it's being documented in real time.

Jane Bozarth also introduced me to the Bill French quote "Email is where knowledge goes to die." When one person shares crucial experience with another person in an organization, it benefits only that single recipient. When experience is blogged internally, or people post and answer questions on a forum, or when people make YouTube videos of how to perform a procedural task, then that knowledge benefits a much wider audience. Learning and development people shouldn't over-engineer the process, but they can make time, technology, and space available for people to share.

Typically, each person has had to learn the tacit skills through experience (which is *very* costly), but the company's training manager has been trying to figure out ways to help everyone learn from each other's experience. One day, she saw a few people gathered around Mila's desk while she walked Hiro through a problem budget. Even some of the experienced people were interested in hearing about it. To facilitate sharing, she's now set up monthly brown bag lunches. Each month, an experienced person opens up a recent project budget and talks through what worked, what didn't work, and what they would do differently next time. Sometimes the meetings are in person, and sometimes they are done remotely using a web meeting platform. One of the best ways to promote informal/social learning is to see where it's already happening and figure out how to support or amplify it.

Formal	Informal / Social
Hiro gets a monthly meeting invite to the budget brown bags.	The training manager schedules the time but doesn't impose any other structure. Sometimes people share recent budgets, and sometimes they bring in current problem budgets so the group can help come up with solutions.

GOAL 4: MANAGE AND TROUBLESHOOT

Next, Hiro needs to learn to manage budgets throughout the project and to troubleshoot cost overruns that may occur. Although in theory he knows the process for managing a budget from week to week, in actuality many unforeseen issues crop up throughout.

Fortunately, Hiro has access to Mila for help. In addition, the other experienced staff have been really encouraged by the knowledge-sharing going on in the brown bag sessions, and they have asked the training manager to set up an internal online discussion forum so they can continue some of the conversations. When Hiro has a problem or an issue, he can post it in the discussion area, and he usually gets a response by the end of the day. This is particularly helpful when he's dealing with material or technology that he's unfamiliar with. His co-workers typically stay on top of new developments in their field and can help him when he has to work with something new.

Formal	Informal / Social
Hiro gets a few guidelines for managing a budget in the initial classroom training.	Hiro asks his mentor or the group for help with issues. As the online group develops, Hiro often finds that he can search and find the answer to his simpler questions in the previous posts.

GOAL 5: DEVELOP FURTHER

As Hiro goes along, he needs to continually develop his project management skills regarding budget and cost controls.

Early on, Hiro is going to feel overwhelmed by the new information, but eventually the learning curve will even out. Hiro will then start to feel like he's getting some mastery of the knowledge in the organization. If he wants to continue developing his skills, he'll probably need to look outside the organization.

He can definitely look at formal solutions like classes, degree programs, conferences, or certifications. All of those are likely to represent a significant investment of time, money, or both.

He can also look at the broader community online: Where are interesting articles being posted? Who is blogging on topics he is interested in? Where are people having interesting conversations?

Tool: Learning Communities

Learning communities—sometimes referred to as communities of practice—can be a tremendous source of information and knowledge and can be much more responsive and up to date than more formal learning sources.

A good learning community doesn't typically just happen, and it often needs care and feeding to grow. One common mistake that I see happening frequently in the field is an "if we build it, they will come" attitude toward learning communities. All too often the conversation focuses on the technology: "Should we get a Twitter clone or a threaded discussion board for our internal social media tool?"

A good community is about and for the participants. The community Elearningheroes.com is run by Tom Kuhlmann and his team to support users of Articulate's elearning authoring software. The strength of the community is that it's not focused on using the software (though you can definitely get help with that); instead, it is focused on helping community members create good elearning and do their jobs better. It's a genuinely useful source of information about elearning design and development, even if you never use their product.

Some people are hesitant about learning communities because they are concerned about people giving wrong or inaccurate answers. The counterargument is that people will give wrong answers even without the learning community—you just won't know about it because it won't be visible to you.

Hiro finds several people on Twitter that
are talking about topics he is interested in
professionally. They link to blogs and articles
that turn out to be very helpful for some
projects that he is working on. He participates
in some Twitter chats and discovers that he
can use a conference hashtag to follow an
event he couldn't attend. He develops rela-
tionships with several people on Twitter
who work in his field, so when he can attend
the conference the following year, he has

several acquaintances he can interact with at the event. He also begins blogging
his own development journey, which gains him a small following.

Formal	Informal / Social
Hiro attends a professional conference.	Hiro interacts with people from his social networks at the conference, and daily or weekly online.

Communities are Living Entities

Learning communities are not machines or technologies that can be turned on by flipping a
switch. A learning community has to grow up organically. This can happen naturally, but
much more frequently a planned community needs a community manager who can tend it
by organizing and moderating the community, by setting up events, and by enlisting con-
federates to ensure there is some initial activity.

Amy Jo Kim, who wrote the excellent and highly recommended *Community Building for the
Web,* talks about how the experience needs to change for community participants over time.

She talks about how each of the different levels needs something different from a community:

- Novices need onboarding. They need to be welcomed, given some goals to achieve, and
  introduced to the way the community functions.
- Regular participants need fresh content, activities, and people to interact with.
- Masters need exclusive activities and access to content and abilities that regular
  participants don't have.

Tool: Curation

When you find someone on Twitter or another social network who always links to the really interesting articles, you are benefiting from their curation skills. Curation can take a number of different forms, but given the tsunami of information we encounter nearly every day, it's becoming an increasingly important skill.

Curation could be the ability to filter or identify the really interesting information in the sea of noisy data. It could be the ability to collect and caption certain pieces of information so that a reader can see how it all fits together. It might be the ability to aggregate all the relevant resources into a single location for easy access. It could be organizing disparate content around a theme, or grouping things to provide context.

Learning design may involve curating materials for your learners, or it may involve identifying or supporting other curators as a resource for your audience.

Tool: Personal Learning Networks

I sometimes find myself explaining the vast difference between my professional network before and after Twitter. Before Twitter, my network consisted primarily of co-workers or classmates. All excellent people, but a fairly small group. Some of my contacts had the same interests that I did. Because we'd worked together or attended the same classes, we had an overlapping body of knowledge.

After Twitter, I know *many* more people, and it's much easier to find the people who get nerdy about the same things I do. I also have access to people with expertise very different from my own. In fact, I only feel like I can write even an introductory chapter on social and informal learning because of all I've learned from my extended personal learning network (PLN).

I frequently teach instructional design workshops for elearning, and I've noticed a consistent theme. I frequently have participants who describe themselves as the one-person elearning shop in their organization. They are the only person in their organization who does what they do, and they are so happy to get to the workshop and talk to other elearning designers. It always makes me a little sad that they've felt so isolated given the vast, vibrant, and welcoming learning communities that exist online.

A PLN doesn't have to be based on Twitter; that just happens to be the platform that worked best for me. It can be whichever community works for you. It doesn't even have to be online—it could be people from local professional organizations. Helping learners find and connect to their own learning communities is another important tool in the learning design toolbox.

SUMMARY

- Most of the learning in your organization probably happens *outside* the classroom.
- Formal learning works best for content that is explicit and stable. Content that is tacit or that changes rapidly is often difficult to incorporate into formal learning.
- Highly complex or variable problems may require the flexibility of an informal or social solution, such as a mentor, a coach, or advice from a community of practice.
- Learning communities cannot be forced and are not about the technology. Instead, they often need to be nurtured or encouraged over time.
- To best focus your efforts for social or informal learning, try to identify the things people are *already* doing and figure out ways to support them.
- While it's always great if one person helps another person, that help can be useful to many more people if it happens "out loud" (e.g., on a message board) so that others can also benefit.
- Activities like curation and the development of a personal learning network are becoming increasingly important not just for learners but also for learning designers.

REFERENCES

Bingham, Tony and Marcia Conner. 2010. *The New Social Learning: A Guide to Transforming Organizations Through Social Media*. ASTD Press and Berrett-Koehler.

Bozarth, Jane. 2014. *Show Your Work*. Pfeiffer.

Brown, J. S., A. Collins, and P. Duguid. 1989. "Situated Cognition and the Culture of Learning." *Educational Researcher* 18: 32–42.

Cross, Jay. 2006. *Informal Learning: Rediscovering the Natural Pathways That Inspire Innovation and Performance*. Pfeiffer.

Duty Calls, XKCD. Retrieved on August 29, 2015, from https://xkcd.com/386.

"Email Is Where Knowledge Goes to Die" Retrieved on August 30, 2015, from http://ipadcto.com/2011/02/28/email-is-where-knowledge-goes-to-die dated 2/28/11.

Kim, Amy Jo. Gamification Workshop. Retrieved on September 7, 2015, from http://www.slideshare.net/amyjokim/gamification-workshop-2010. Published on Nov 19, 2010.

Kim, Amy Jo. 2000. *Community Building on the Web*. Berkeley: Peachpit Press.

DESIGN FOR ENVIRONMENT

(IN WHICH WE LEARN THAT
SOME STOVES ARE SMARTER THAN OTHERS,
AND THAT PROXIMITY MATTERS)

ENVIRONMENT GAPS

One of my very first professional jobs was doing training for the customer service call center in a financial services company (not that exciting, but a really good learning experience).

The job of being a customer service rep (CSR) in this call center was pretty demanding. Not only did you deal with grumpy people all day, but you also had to coax customer information from several different computer systems.

The reps had to constantly flip back and forth between the accounting systems, the credit systems, and the customer records systems for four different divisions, and most of these systems didn't talk to each other. Their computer screens looked like this:

As you can imagine, it took a while to get really good at this. We figured that, despite our best training efforts, it took about six months before a rep was really comfortable navigating all the systems and answering most customer questions.

It was also an entry-level position, and due to a lot of expansion, reps could often transfer out to other, better-paid positions in the company pretty rapidly.

So it worked kind of like this:

Amount of time to get a CSR up to speed = about 6 months

Amount time to before a CSR transferred out of the department = about 6 months

You can see the difficulty here.

While there were undoubtedly many things we could've done to improve the training experience, that wasn't really the problem. There were too many weird exceptions, and too many instances where reps had to learn and remember bizarre strings of procedures to get the right information to answer the customer's question.

Actually, it was kind of amazing that the reps were able to get good at their jobs at all, given the difficulty of the environment. That they did was a testament to practice and determination.

The real gaps weren't in knowledge or skills or motivation. The real gaps were in the environment. That's what we needed to fix.

KNOWLEDGE IN THE WORLD

Donald Norman, in his fantastic, classic design book *The Design of Everyday Things*, has a chapter called "Knowledge in the Head and in the World." In it, he talks about taking the burden off of memory (knowledge in the head) and putting that information into the environment (knowledge in the world).

The example he gave is his stovetop, which was set up somewhat similar to this:

There are four burners and four dials, but can you tell which dial lights which burner? At best, you can narrow it down to one of two options, and then you a) take the time to figure out which one it is each time you use the stove, b) memorize which is which, or c) guess, and hope you don't set anything on fire.

Norman then points out that there are ways to design stoves where you don't have to remember anything. For example, can you tell which dial goes with which burner on this stovetop?

Changing the design of the environment can make knowledge or skills gaps disappear. By taking the knowledge and embedding it in the world, we can vastly reduce the amount of information we ask our learners to pick up and carry around.

LEARNING THE *RIGHT* THINGS

It's not practical or appropriate to take *the entire* burden off the learners, but there are things that both people and technology are good at and bad at, and they are mostly not the same things.

Things That (Most) People Are Bad At	Things That (Most) People Are Good At
Differential calculus	Walking in the woods
Loan calculations and amortizations	Understanding what other people are saying
Retaining and retrieving large strings of information	Recognizing and responding to emotions

Things That Technology Is Bad At	Things That Technology Is Good At
Walking in the woods	Differential calculus
Understanding what other people are saying	Loan calculations and amortizations
Recognizing and responding to emotions	Retaining and retrieving large strings of information

Improving the environment is about clearing out as much of the stuff that learners don't really need to carry around in their heads, and instead letting them focus on the things that only they are able to do.

PROXIMITY MATTERS

One of the things you need to consider when putting knowledge into the world is the proximity of the knowledge to the task.

By this I mean, how far from the task does the learner have to go to get the knowledge?

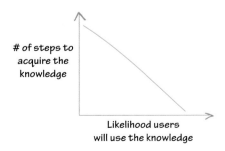

Admittedly, that chart is my estimation (and is not based on actual data), but if the learner has to find an instruction manual, open it to the table of contents, scan for the subject, turn to the section, consult the index, and finally find the information they are looking for, then they are probably going to skip it and ask the person sitting next to them instead—a valid strategy, unless the person next to them doesn't know or would prefer not to be interrupted.

The closer you can get the knowledge to the place the user is going to use it, the more likely they'll actually do so. We'll look at a few different ways to put knowledge into the environment, based on their proximity to the task:

- Resources
- Triggers or prompts
- Embedded behaviors

PUTTING RESOURCES IN THE WORLD

There are many ways to put knowledge resources into the environment. It's beyond the scope of this book to go into huge detail on this, but we'll just take a look at a few examples (for more on this topic, Allison Rossett's books on job aids are excellent resources).

JOB AIDS

Job aids are typically prompts, instructions, or memory aids that are readily available to help people accomplish tasks.

Here's one of my favorite job aids:

This

This unimportant-looking yellow tag on my jumper cables gives me a quick reminder about how not to electrocute myself while jumping a car battery. I've probably jumped a few dozen batteries over the years, but it's typically been several months to years between instances, and I find it very reassuring to be able to consult the little tag right there.

This is a great example of the importance of proximity. If there weren't a little tag attached to my jumper cables, I'd probably be tempted to just wing it rather than try to get the information elsewhere.

A colleague of mine, Dave Ferguson, talks about how job aids can act as *training wheels,* which he describes as something to "guide the novice so that he produces results similar to those of an expert without having to internalize all the knowledge the expert has" (Ferguson 2009).

Dave goes on to explain that job aids, like an airline's preflight checklist, can also act as *guard rails* to "protect you from incorrect or unsafe performance."

The jumper cables do a little of both for me. I could probably do it right without the tag, but it's nice to have the reminder, and I check my performance against the instructions to avoid the aforementioned electrocution.

In the "nice to have a reminder" category, reference keys can provide simple, useful information that some people might really need and that might just make others feel more "supported," knowing they can double-check themselves at a time when they may not be thinking clearly. For example, the simple icons on a map legend or a wall placard in an airport may seem obvious when you think clearly about them, but more unusual ones may require explanation.

Here are a few other types of job aids:

- **Decision trees** If a process has very specific and predetermined decision points, then giving people a logical, step-by-step way to navigate those decisions can significantly improve learner performance.

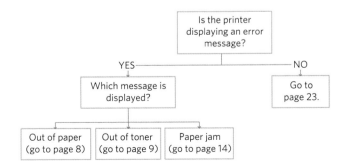

Related to decision trees are process diagrams and even org charts.

- **Reference information**   People aren't good at remembering long sequences of numbers or detailed lists, so providing learners quick, easy access to those types of information can make a big difference in the efficiency of the process.

- **Augmented reality**   An interesting type of job aid that's starting to gain traction is *augmented reality*, which puts a virtual information "layer" over the real world and can be viewed using virtual-reality headsets or the camera on mobile devices.

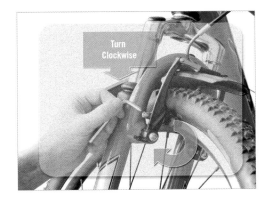

SUPPLY CACHING

When your learners are first learning something, they can be overwhelmed with detail, so figuring out ways to cache some of that information and provide it later can be useful.

For example, I've been trying to learn Adobe Illustrator so I can edit the graph-ics that appear in this book. I'm still a novice (I know enough to break things), but I love watching experts use the program. A graphic designer friend of mine is a wizard at Illustrator, and when he uses it his fingers dance all over the key-board. He knows dozens of keyboard shortcuts that he learned to speed up his performance.

Trying to learn keyboard shortcuts while I try to master the basics of Illustrator is probably too much for me, but as I go along I will want that information.

A common, easy job aid in the training world is a card that has the keyboard shortcuts on it, which I could keep at my desk.

Many software makers have done a nice thing, though, that leaves that infor-mation in an even handier place:

Basically, this information is placed as close as possible to the actual behav-ior—while I am in the act of using the Edit menu to select the "Paste in Place" command, I have an informational prompt that lets me know there's a shortcut key for that particular command, if I would care to use it in the future.

Another example of this that I've always liked is in the interface of the tax soft-ware I used to use. Whatever page of the tax entry program I was on would have handy questions in the side column, such as "What is the alternative mini-mum tax?" I could look it up, but the real strength of that particular interface was that it typically showed only the five or six questions that were most rel-evant at the time. Another nice tactic was to put the message "This is unusual" next to obscure tax questions so I would know that they were probably not relevant to me. This program has also started crowdsourcing by capturing and displaying other users' questions and answers. Leveraging your learners' knowl-edge through wikis or forums can be an invaluable source of information.

PUTTING PROMPTS/TRIGGERS IN THE WORLD

We talked in Chapter 9 about Gollwitzer's implementation intentions. Basically, you create a script for yourself that says, "if X happens, I will do Y." So if you are trying to quit smoking and you find yourself craving a cigarette because you are bored, you use your predetermined implementation intention to deal with that (*"If I crave a cigarette because I'm bored, I'll play Candy Crush on my phone"*).

The way this relates to environment is that you then figure out a way to put the triggers in the real world. Are there ways to take the prompts or triggers from implementation intentions and give them a physical presence in your learners' environments?

This is already being done for some things:

This is both a good and bad example. Some research (e.g., Johnson 2003) suggests that handwashing signs do increase the number of people who wash their hands, but that it clearly doesn't work with everybody. It's also likely that people habituate to these signs pretty quickly (one way to offset habituation is to use novelty—for example, Mr. T could remind you to wash your hands one week, and a *Schoolhouse Rock* character could prompt you the next).

Still, prompts in the environment can increase behavior, and it's likely that having your learners create their own prompts would be a more effective way to encourage behavior.

Another of my favorite examples of putting a prompt into the environment is this example from the pretzel shops that you often find in shopping malls. They have on their countertops pretzel-shaped markings that look kind of like this:

This handy guide is built right into the countertop. You just roll the dough out to the length and thickness of one of the lines (for larger and smaller pretzels) and then wrap it on top of the appropriate pretzel shape.

This is an example of a prompt that not only triggers the behavior but also provides guidance on how to perform the task. Experienced pretzel-makers probably ignore the markings, but the guides are an excellent example of how to embed "training wheels" into the environment for new employees.

PUTTING BEHAVIORS IN THE WORLD

Have you ever seen the person in the small food stand or diner who just *knows* how long things take? Maybe she can start a drink pouring at the soda machine, turn to ring a customer, and know exactly how long she has before she needs to turn around and keep the cup from overfilling. That's the sign of an expert who really knows their job and has internalized that knowledge over time.

More common these days is the evidence of that knowledge being embedded into the world.

The type of soda machine shown below is pretty common. The employee can put in the cup and just press a single button for small, medium, or large.

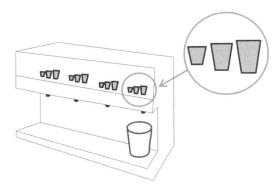

The point is that environment is a very powerful regulator of behavior, and if people aren't doing the right thing, it's important to look at ways to improve the environment.

Always ask these questions:

- Can we make the process simpler?
- Can we make the system better?
- What barriers are keeping people from succeeding?

You want to walk through the process step by step looking for problems. You particularly want to keep an eye peeled for frustration points, because the more you can do to smooth out the journey, the more likely your learners are to succeed.

Ask "why are we doing it that way?" at each step. If you hear the words "that's the process" or "that's how we've always done it," then that should be a big, screaming alarm telling you to scrutinize that step and make sure it's really necessary rather than just a habit or tradition.

THE BIG QUESTION

Here's the crucial question to ask yourself when designing for environment:

> **ASK:** What's everything else we could do (besides training) that will allow learners to succeed?

For this, I recommend a full-on, whiteboard-scribbling, multi-colored sticky note, no idea is a bad idea, free-for-all brainstorm session. Then consider all those solutions. If laminating wall-size posters, or making cookies, or flying in experts, or hiring an on-site masseuse, or setting up a wiki, or buying everyone Magic 8 Balls (as decision-making aids, of course) will help the process, then consider the cost benefit of those notions.

To get more detail, you should also ask "what could we do beforehand to make people more ready?" and "what could we do afterward to reinforce?"

SUMMARY

- Instead of trying to put all the knowledge into the learners' heads, try to figure out whether some of the knowledge can be put into the environment instead.
- Activities that are particularly difficult for humans to master are good candidates for embedding into the environment.
- Proximity matters—try to get the knowledge as close to the behavior as possible.
- When designing for environment, remember that recognizing the right option is easier than recalling it.
- Don't just teach learners how to do a process; look at the process to see whether there's any way to streamline it to make it simpler and easier to perform.

REFERENCES

Ferguson, David. 2009. "Job Aids: Training Wheels and Guard Rails." *Dave's Whiteboard, March 31, 2009*. www.daveswhiteboard.com/archives/1939.

Gollwitzer, P. M. 2006. "Successful Goal Pursuit." *Psychological Science Around the World* 1: 143–159, Q. Jing, H. Zhang, and K. Zhang, Eds. Philadelphia: Psychology Press.

Gollwitzer, P. M., K. Fujita, and G. Oettingen. 2004. "Planning and the Implementation of Goals." *Handbook of Self-Regulation: Research, Theory, and Applications*, R. F. Baumeister and K. D. Vohs, Eds. New York: Guilford Press.

Jeffery, Robert W. and Jennifer Utter. 2003. "The Changing Environment and Population Obesity in the United States." *Obesity Research* 11, DOI: 10.1038/oby.2003.221.

Johnson, H. D., D. Sholoscky, K. L. Gabello, R. V. Ragni, and N. M. Ogonosky. 2003. "Gender Differences in Handwashing Behavior Associated with Visual Behavior Prompts." *Perceptual and Motor Skills* 97: 805–810.

Norman, Donald. 1990. *The Design of Everyday Things*. New York: Doubleday Business.

12

DESIGNING EVALUATION

(IN WHICH WE LEARN THAT A, B, C, AND D ARE NOT YOUR ONLY OPTIONS)

THE CHALLENGE OF DOING GOOD EVALUATION

WHAT DOES LEARNING EVALUATION LOOK LIKE?

If you close your eyes and picture learning assessment, there's a decent chance you'll picture something like this:

The most common form of formal assessment is everybody's favorite: the multiple-choice question. We've all answered more multiple-choice questions than we can possibly remember.

If we use so many of them, they must be the good way to do learning assessment, right? Well, they have a few main advantages:

- They are efficient to write, administer, and score.
- Grading is objective.
- They are consistent; everyone who takes the test can have the same experience.

OK, so what *isn't* on that list? Oh yeah—there's pretty much nothing on there about the learning advantages for *the person taking the test*.

Multiple-choice tests aren't really about making the learner better at what they need to do. They are about making test administration efficient and consistent. If your main goal is testing and assessment, then that's fine. You've got yourself a model.

But here's the thing. Mainly what you learn from multiple-choice tests is how good the learner is at…taking multiple-choice tests. You don't want to hand someone the keys to the helicopter just because they passed the 100-question multiple-choice test on the history of helicopter flight.

WHAT ARE WE TRYING TO MEASURE?

To do evaluation well, you should start by defining what you are trying to evaluate. Some of the things you might want to know include:

- Does my learning design function well?
- Are the learners actually learning the right things?
- Can the learners actually do the right things?
- Are the learners actually *doing* the right things when they go back to the real world?

Let's take a look at each of these questions and the kinds of evaluation you can use to answer them.

DOES IT WORK?

When you begin evaluation, the first question you want to answer is, "Does my learning design function well?"—basically, does the darn thing work?

This leads to all sorts of follow-up questions:

- Do I have enough content? Too much content?
- Are the instructions clear? Do people know what to do?
- Does the timing work, or does it go on way too long?
- Are learners engaged, or are they so bored they'd rather chew off a limb than listen any further?
- Are learners keeping up with the pace, or are they getting frustrated and left behind?

The best way you answer these questions = *Watch actual learners use your design.*

This could mean watching how learners react in a class, or how they use an elearning course, or what they do with other types of learning materials. We discussed this briefly in Chapter 2, but testing things out with actual users is really the only way to know what works and what doesn't.

Both experience and good design make it easier to create a learning experience that works pretty well out of the box, but even the best learning experience has some hiccups the first time it's executed:

This kind of thing is going to happen, so it's probably better if it happens with a nice, tolerant pilot group who know that you're launching something for the first time. This is something we do automatically with instructor-led classes. I often ask groups of training facilitators if any of them have ever failed to make adjustments between the first and second time they taught a class. No one has ever raised their hand. Of course you would make adjustments after the first time you teach something, so you should plan for a pilot as part of your design process.

TESTING DIGITAL RESOURCES

Other types of learning materials—self-study materials or elearning or digital support resources—often get released without any kind of user review. Usually they are just reviewed by stakeholders or subject matter experts, which is a necessary part of the process, but getting feedback only from people who already know the topic well is a problem.

When you design a learning experience, it's easy to get tunnel vision. You've been working for weeks or months, parsing out all the messy pieces of content and figuring out how to organize them, and finally it's all making sense to you:

But your learners will be starting from scratch, and things that are now perfectly apparent to you will be a muddled mass of confusion to them. But you (and all the other experts and stakeholders) have lost the ability to see the confusion, because you've been so close to the material for so long. You need fresh, outside eyes from your target audience to really know what works and what doesn't work.

The good news is that it has gotten very easy to test online digital resources. The steps are as follows:

1. **Recruit some learners.** You don't need very many. The industry rule of thumb is that five or six end users are plenty. I've done user testing with two or three people and still gotten value from it. There are agencies that will help you recruit users, but when I needed middle-school teachers, for example, I asked friends and family to get volunteers.
2. **Arrange a web meeting with a learner.** You want to interact with each learner individually so that you can pay close attention to how they interact with your materials.
3. **Explain the process.** When they are logged in to the web meeting, explain that you are testing the digital resource (not them) and that they can't do anything wrong. Ask them to talk aloud as they move through the elearning course or the digital resource.
4. **Ask them to share their screen.** Have them share their screen via the web meeting application, and have them access the elearning course or resource. Ask them to go through it or to perform specific tasks.
5. **Watch what they do.** If you have permission, record the session and watch what they do. See where they get frustrated or stuck, and see where they miss things. Don't help them unless they are really stuck (you won't be there for all the rest of your learners to explain things).

That's it. Repeat the process with three to five other learners, and you will learn an enormous amount about how learning functions. Make changes and repeat the testing process as often as you can manage. You can also do these same steps in person if that is more convenient.

Steve Krug's excellent (and entertaining) books *Don't Make Me Think* and *Rocket Surgery Made Easy* are essential reading if you are designing and testing any kind of digital resource. Usability.gov is another great (and free!) resource for user testing materials and guidelines.

USING SURVEYS

"This whole user testing thing sounds complicated. Can't we just give them a survey after they take the course to find out if it works?"

If you've studied instructional design, you are probably familiar with the Kirkpatrick levels of evaluation. Level 1 evaluation is "Reaction—To what degree participants react favorably to the training" (Kirkpatrick 2015).

Frequently, it gets measured with something like this:

Level 1: Reaction Survey	Strongly Agree				Strongly Disagree	
Class						
The material presented was useful to me.	5	4	3	2	1	N/A
The material was presented in an engaging way.	5	4	3	2	1	N/A
The instructor managed to get through all 117 PowerPoint slides without passing out from exhaustion.	5	4	3	2	1	N/A

I have no problem with asking people after the class/course/resource whether they liked it. Sure, why not ask? This is probably the single most common form of evaluation for adult learners, because (like multiple-choice questions) it's the easiest and quickest to do.

If you choose to measure reaction, here are a few things you should consider:

- **This data tends to be collected after the whole learning resource has been completed, proofread, checked, and polished.** This means that it's really hard to go back and change things that aren't working. If you can get reactions (along with user testing results) earlier in the development process, you are much more likely to be able to correct things before it gets too far.
- **Try to keep it short.** I've noticed a trend toward shorter customer satisfactions surveys (one to three questions), to which I can only say *hallelujah!* Try to keep yourself to no more than four questions, and have at least one question be an open-ended text field in which people can write their own feedback.
- **Recognize the limitations**. This kind of survey will most likely alert you to problems. If your audience is unhappy, you probably need to take action. What this type of survey will not do is tell if you things are really working. You could get positive responses because people didn't really understand, or because they wanted to be nice, or because you asked the question in just the right way. There are ways to maximize the efficacy of reaction surveys (Thalheimer 2015), but to really understand whether the learning experience is effective, we need to look at other measures.

ARE THEY LEARNING?

There are whole books on the topic of test construction, and I won't be able to address all the issues with measuring learning, but I want to discuss a few considerations.

RECOGNITION VERSUS RECALL

We discussed the issue of recognition versus recall in Chapter 4, but it's worth discussing here too.

Take a look at this question. What do you think the right answer is?

> You have an angry customer demanding that you reverse a charge on her account, but you don't have the authority to do so.
>
> What do you say?
>
> A) "I'm sorry ma'am, but that's the policy."
>
> B) "Only a manager can do that."
>
> C) "Ma'am, I understand why you would be upset about an incorrect charge."
>
> D) "Of course we'll take care of that right away!"

You don't have to know all that much about customer service to figure out that answers A and B will cause customer rage and that D is just wrong.

So if a learner answers this question correctly, what does that tell you about what they learned? It tells you that they can apply basic logic to a situation, but it tells you very little about their customer service knowledge.

Recognition isn't a bad thing, and it's often a necessary first step in understanding a topic, but it only gets you so far.

A recall-based question would be much better.

> You have an angry customer demanding that you reverse a charge on her account, but you don't have the authority to do so.
>
> What do you say? (Write your answer in the space provided.)

The problem with recall questions is that a human has to look at them to judge whether the answers are right or wrong, which is a much more labor-intensive process than letting a computer grade the choice of A, B, C, or D.

If learners need to recall their answers in the real world, you should use recall-based assessment whenever you can, but sometimes it's just not an option. Sometimes, the only available tool in your toolbox is recognition-based assessment. How can you use it most effectively?

There are ways to make recognition questions better:

- **Make them scenario-based.** If the questions are part of a bigger, context-rich scenario based on the real dilemmas people face on the job, then right answers will often be more challenging to identify, and learners will have context cues that will help them transfer the idea to their work environments.
- **Have lots of options.** This is a fairly blunt solution, but if you are asking a question about what particular tool a repair person should use to replace the solenoid valve on a dishwashing machine, they will have to think more critically to select it from a visual showing all the standard tools in their toolbox, rather than selecting one answer from a list of four in a multiple-choice question.

- **Don't use wrong answers.** The format for multiple-choice questions is typically one right answer and two or three wrong answers. But if the choices are one pretty good answer, one semi-mediocre answer, one great answer, and one OK answer, then finding the best answer becomes much more challenging. It can be very difficult to write one plausible distractor (wrong answer). Writing three plausible distractors is sometimes just not possible. You can also weight answers—for example, a really good answer could be worth 10 points, but an OK answer might only be worth 3 points.

SO RECOGNITION CAN WORK?

Recognition-based testing is still a limited format, and it really only works well for knowledge-based gaps. If your learning objectives are all about salespeople knowing the right answers to customer product questions, it's not too difficult to figure out how to use recognition-based test questions to assess that. Recall or performance are probably still better options, though, particularly when we start to assess skills. We'll talk about performance feedback next.

CAN THE LEARNERS ACTUALLY DO THE RIGHT THINGS?

If you are assessing a learner's ability to recall or generate answers, or their ability to perform a skill, you need assessment that has them *perform*. Their performance should then be evaluated.

Basically, you need to do these two things:

- Have the learner perform the task.
- Give them useful feedback.

That's it.

OK, it's a little more complicated than that, but that should be the heart of most learning assessment.

So what are the issues? Well, first you need to figure out who will be providing the feedback, and next you will need to figure out how to make sure that the feedback is valuable and consistent.

PROVIDING FEEDBACK

If the popularity of recognition-based evaluation is because feedback is easy and consistent, the challenge of recall evaluation is that feedback can be difficult and inconsistent.

The more complex the performance, the less likely that there is a single "right" answer, which means that evaluating can't be handled by a computer or a testing assistant with an answer key. Instead, you have to have a human being who can read or watch the performance and give meaningful feedback.

And your evaluators need to have sufficient expertise not only in the subject area but also in evaluating and providing feedback. I might know how to play tennis, but that doesn't mean I know how to evaluate tennis performance in others or how to communicate that feedback in a clear and useful way.

If it's too costly to have an expert reviewer, some possible alternatives include:

- **Peer-to-peer feedback.** When there aren't sufficient expert resources, it can be possible to arrange for students to give each other feedback. It obviously depends on the task being performed. Some of the online language platforms have used this to help students get feedback on their pronunciation. If I'm an English speaker who wants to learn Lithuanian, I can help a Chinese speaker with her English pronunciation, and in turn I can get help from a Lithuanian student who is using the platform to learn English.

- **Near-peer feedback.** While my tennis skills definitely don't qualify me to give expert-level feedback, my intermediate-level skills could probably enable me to give reasonable feedback to very novice tennis players, particularly if I were given specific guidelines by an expert instructor (e.g.,"Don't let the racket come up above the elbow").

- **Self-evaluation.** You can create opportunities for the learner to self-evaluate by giving them criteria, reflection questions, or examples that they can compare their performance to. I've used the following format in elearning courses when it wasn't possible to provide human feedback:

The learner enters their own response and then submits it to see the checklist and self-evaluate. Next, the learner can click Continue to see the expert versions.

CONSISTENCY

The other issue, of course, is consistency. The more subjective the performance is, the more that the feedback will be in the eye of the beholder.

So if you have human evaluators giving subjective feedback, how do you ensure that there's consistency? Even if all the feedback is coming from the same person, consistency can be an issue. One study found that judges give harsher sentences right before lunch than they do earlier in the day (Danziger 2011), and it's not possible for a grader to remember exactly what logic they used on the first paper when they are grading the forty-first paper.

Tools that you can use to create feedback consistency include checklists and rubrics.

A checklist can be a consistent set of steps or items in a task, or a set of criteria that the learner needs to meet. For example, if you want to evaluate whether or not a new housekeeping staff member has adequately learned to clean hotel rooms, you will give much better feedback if you have a checklist of all the required steps with performance criteria (e.g., "Wiped mirror, leaving streak-free").

A rubric can have the same items, but it will also usually have specific rating criteria to help improve the consistency of scoring. The self-assessment for time management in Chapter 9 is an example of a rubric. Rubrics are frequently developed to make the performance of tacit skills more explicit, as we saw in the Chapter 9 section on designing for habits.

Let's take a look at an example. Think about how you might assess this situation:

SCENARIO: PRESENTATION SKILLS

Imagine you are teaching workshops to small nonprofit organizations about how to create and deliver fundraising presentations. You've told them specific elements that need to be included in a good fundraising appeal, taught them principles for creating a polished and attractive presentation deck (font, color, images, slide layout), and modeled good speaking technique. How could you evaluate what your participants have learned?

—TAKE A MOMENT TO CONSIDER WHAT YOU WOULD DO BEFORE MOVING ON—

Design solution
Clearly the performance will have to be the learner creating a presentation deck and presenting it. The instructor should use a checklist of the elements to provide feedback. The instructor could also develop a rubric around the principles of creating good slides and a polished deck, or at least provide specific feedback on how the learner used each of the elements (font, color, images, slide layout). In addition to evaluator feedback, peer-to-peer feedback could be a good option for the evaluation of the presentation delivery, or the instructor could video-record each presentation and encourage the learners to self-evaluate using the criteria they were taught. ▪

USE YOUR OBJECTIVES

If you've used the criteria from Chapter 2 for developing learning objectives (would it happen in the real world, and can you tell if they've done it), then those learning objectives should point directly to the performance required for evaluation.

Let's look at a few of those objectives:

- Learner should be able to identify all the criteria necessary to select the correct product for the client.
- Learner should be able to create a website that works on the five most common browsers.
- Learner should be able to identify whether a complaint meets the definition of sexual harassment, and state the reasons why.

The performance for each one of these is spelled out in the learning objectives, though you still have to determine how you will evaluate that performance.

One trick that experienced learning designers use is to create the evaluation *before* building the learning experience so that they have a clear road map for the learning design.

Can we just let them test out?

One question I hear frequently is

"Can't we just let them test out, so they don't have to go back over material they already know?"

The answer to this is a resounding

"YES, but..."

"Yes," because it's great to be sensitive to your learners' individual needs and experiences, and "but" because it's hard to do this well. The suggestion I most commonly hear is to have multiple-choice questions at the front of the course (you see where this is going), but that probably only works if the learning objectives are knowledge based.

So the answer is yes, you can let them test out *if* you are confident that your testing mechanism is robust enough to really assess their ability.

ARE THE LEARNERS ACTUALLY DOING THE RIGHT THINGS?

Now that we've talked about some of the issues in evaluating learning and ability (roughly Kirkpatrick Level 2, for those keeping track), we get to our last and most important question.

Are the learners actually *doing* the right things when they go back to the real world?

In my experience, this tends to be the least measured element in adult learning. It's not hard to understand why. Figuring this out can be a costly undertaking if your organization isn't already collecting performance metrics.

If your organization does regularly collect metrics, this isn't so bad. Let's say you are creating a training on how to sell water softeners for your commercial plumbing service. You probably know how many water softeners were sold in May. If you roll the training out at the beginning of June and sales double, you can be pretty confident that the training accomplished something.

If you want to be sure that it isn't due to some other variable (a groundbreaking exposé on the tragedy of hard water, or the rollout of a supernewshiny water softener), you can do A/B testing. To do that, you split your sales force in half (groups A and B) and have only group A take the training. If group A outperforms group B, then you have good reason to believe the training was effective. If the training was effective, you can roll out the training to group B after the test period.

But what if your organization isn't already collecting those metrics? For example, what if you are creating a course to help managers get better at feedback, but there are no manager-effectiveness measures in place? Or what if you don't have that much access to learners after they go back to the real world, like the students in the public workshop on how to conduct usability tests?

There are two strategies you can look at:

- Observation
- Success cases

OBSERVATION

If you lack organizational metrics, direct observation is probably the most effective method. If you do a training that emphasizes wearing safety glasses on the shop floor, then you should go down to the shop floor and count the number of people wearing safety glasses before and after the training.

But what about our manager feedback example? That's not quite so visible and, therefore, not quite so easy to count. How can we measure whether or not that's happening in the world?

One option is to use the checklists or rubrics you created for evaluation, and modify them for use by either the learners' supervisors or the learners themselves. Supervisors often want to help develop their people, but they are busy, and a format that makes it relatively easy for them to do observation and feedback can sometimes make a real difference.

If observation of the entire population just isn't practical, cohort observation could be an option. If you are training 12,000 nurses how to use a piece of medical technology, it's probably impossible to observe the whole population, but you could observe two or three groups of 20 nurses and use that data to inform your practice.

You can look for other signals that may indicate whether the training is effective. For example, would employee retention be better if managers were better at giving feedback? Would there be fewer calls to the help desk if the new hire training for service techs were successful? Would the rates of infection go down if the handwashing training were successful?

I saw a presentation a few years ago in which the training department attached Google Analytics to their internal help and support pages so that they could tell which pages were accessed frequently and which had never been accessed. While this wasn't conclusive proof of efficacy, it did help them understand the impact they were having.

QUALITATIVE INTERVIEWS AND CASE STUDIES

So if these methods sound great but ultimately aren't practical for your situation, interviews and case studies could be feasible methods.

Basically, can you call up a half dozen of your learners four to six weeks after the learning event and talk to them about what is working and not working? If you get them to tell you stories about application, you can learn much more from the conversation than you can from a survey or a test score.

If you need a more formalized approach, the Success Case Method, by Robert Brinkerhoff, is a good option. Essentially, the steps are:

- Determine what the impact of the learning should be for the organization.
- Send out a very short survey a short time after the training to identify who is using the learned material and who is not.
- Conduct interviews with a handful of the most successful and least successful users.

If you have the email addresses of your attendees, you can follow up using this method regardless of the circumstances. Even if you talk to only a half dozen of your learners, the information will be invaluable. There is more detail about implementing this method in Brinkerhoff's book *The Success Case Method*.

The crucial piece is to figure out how to get feedback into your own learning design practice. How do you know that what you are doing is effective? Some of it probably isn't, but if you don't have feedback coming back into the system, you'll never be sure what is working and what isn't.

SUMMARY

- Test your learning on a few users ahead of time so you can smooth out the rough edges before it goes out to your entire population.
- Use recall- or performance-based assessment whenever you can.
- Surveys can give you useful information, but keep them short and give learners some space to write their own responses about what worked and what didn't. Surveys probably shouldn't be your only form of evaluation.
- If you use multiple-choice testing, try to use scenario-based questions that require your learners to apply what they've learned.
- Have people perform, and give them feedback.
- Peer evaluation or self-evaluation can also provide useful feedback.
- Use checklists or rubrics to make feedback more useful and consistent.
- Observation and interviews can provide feedback to you as the designer about what is and is not working in the learning experience.
- Look for the signals in your organization (e.g., the number of customer service calls) that can give you an idea of whether things are changing.

REFERENCES

Brinkerhoff, Robert O. 2003. *The Success Case Method: Find Out Quickly What's Working and What's Not*. Berrett-Koehler.

Danziger, Shai, Jonathan Levav and Liora Avnaim-Pesso. "Extraneous Factors in Judicial Decisions." *PNAS* April 26, 2011. 108 (17).

New World Kirkpatrick Model. Retrieved October 13, 2015, from www.kirkpatrickpartners.com/OurPhilosophy/TheNewWorldKirkpatrickModel/tabid/303.

Thalheimer, Will. 2015. "Performance-Focused Smile Sheets: A Radical Rethinking of a Dangerous Art Form." www.SmileSheets.com.

CONCLUSION

(IN WHICH WE SAY, "THANK YOU!")

Small children are natural learners—they just suck information out of their environment through curiosity and play.

Somewhere along the way, we lose that. We learn that learning is serious business and that it's hard and effortful. Learning designers have an opportunity to defy that notion and create marvelous, interesting, relevant learning environments. We can't *make* anybody learn, but we can make much better learning environments for them and help each learner be the hero of their own learning journey.

If you've read this whole book, it's probably because you want to make better, more effective learning. I sincerely thank you for wanting to create the best possible experience for your learners.

It seems fitting to end the book with a quotation from the fantastic Kathy Sierra, who has been hugely influential on me as a learning designer:

> *"Kicking ass is more fun regardless of the task. It's more fun to know more. It's more fun to be able to do more. It's more fun to be able to help others do more."*

INDEX